Rosie:
My Rufous
HUMMINGBIRD

A beautiful bird with a feisty, endearing personality.

Rosie:
My Rufous
HUMMINGBIRD

ARNETTE HEIDCAMP

with photographs and drawings by the author

CROWN PUBLISHERS, INC.

NEW YORK

Published by Crown Publishers, Inc., 201 East 50th Street, New York, New York 10022. Member of the Crown Publishing Group.

Random House, Inc. New York, Toronto, London, Sydney, Auckland

CROWN is a trademark of Crown Publishers, Inc.

Manufactured in Hong Kong

Design by Jennifer Harper

Library of Congress Cataloging-in-Publication Data
Heidcamp. Arnette.
Rosie: my rufous hummingbird / Arnette Heidcamp ; with photographs and drawings by the author—1st ed.
p. cm.
1. Hummingbirds as pets. 2. Rufous hummingbird—Biography.
3. Heidcamp, Arnette. I. Title.
SF473.H84H458   1995

636.6—dc20   94-40643
                                                  CIP

ISBN 0-517-70076-X

10   9   8   7   6   5   4   3   2

First, for Rosie,
a beautiful bird and endearing personality
who has brought much happiness to my life

Next, for my husband, George,
and my family

and, finally,
in memory of Rupert

Also by Arnette Heidcamp

A Hummingbird in My House:
The Story of Squeak

Contents

Rosie:
My Rufous
HUMMINGBIRD

Introduction

In the fall of 1988 a young male ruby-throated hummingbird who had failed to migrate appeared in my garden. To save that bird from a certain unnecessary death, I lured him into my sunroom to spend the winter until it became safe to release him the following spring. That bird is the subject of my earlier book, *A Hummingbird in My House: The Story of Squeak*. Having Squeak as a winter guest had been a wonderful experience, one that I shall never forget and one that I never expected to experience again—unless Squeak himself returned, ready to spend another winter. This book is the story of another hummingbird, a species that is exceptionally unusual for my area, who paid me a visit one autumn and then refused to leave—the story of an off-course rufous hummingbird who spent the winter of 1993–1994 as yet another guest in my sunroom.

Since the first book was released I've received many cards, letters, and telephone calls from people who read Squeak's story, asking whether he had returned. I'm sorry to report that he didn't, and I think it would be appropriate here to tell a little about the conclusions I've reached with respect to that question and why.

All who have read Squeak's story know how it

broke my heart when I released him, but another experience has given me some insight into the rubythroat's powerful territorial instincts and has offered a plausible answer about what may have happened with Squeak. In May 1991 a woman turned over to me the care of an adult male ruby-throated hummingbird that five days before had been captured by a cat. The attack caused extensive soft-tissue damage to the muscle that elevates the bird's wing and left it totally incapacitated and in need of constant hand-feeding and related care. The bird hailed from an area about twelve miles away and was delivered to me at my office, ten miles in the other direction. For the first week and a half, Charlie, as I called him, traveled with me to and from work, where he would sit in an open basket on my desk to be hand-fed at regular intervals. After that he was able to maneuver well enough in his basket to reach the feeder on his own. With steady improvement, eventually he was able to generate the lift necessary to get himself out of the basket and that was followed not too long afterward by gliding, very short flights, regular flying, and, finally, hovering. In less than one month after Charlie's episode with the cat, he was flying and hovering and vigorously exploring his surroundings. The only problem Charlie seemed to have was a deformity of one foot that was probably preexisting. Once hovering was perfected and other signs of progress were evident, Charlie began to exhibit an avid interest in the world beyond the sunroom. It soon became apparent that he was close to being ready to be on his own.

Charlie was released on June 26, six weeks after the encounter with the cat. Like Squeak before him, he stopped and checked out the fuchsia under the back porch overhang and then took off. Territorial instincts, as they relate to returning in the spring, are well known. I had been wondering whether he would be following those instincts and whether he would attempt to return to his original breeding territory. His rapid departure answered my question. Much may be said for the rubythroats' territorial instincts and much may be said for their sense of direction as well. After having been taken several miles away from his territory, and after having been driven ten miles each way to work and back every day for more than a week, Charlie still found his regular stomping grounds. Members of the family of the woman who had brought him to me spotted him in their garden. They had been able to positively identify him by his deformed right foot. Charlie was a lucky bird, as the rate of successful rehabilitation and release attempts of songbirds is notoriously low. And that brings us to another lucky hummingbird, Squeak. On the basis of what happened with Charlie, I would speculate that Squeak returned to wherever he had been before he appeared in this garden. Of course, one can merely theorize about what happened ultimately to any of them. You do your best to change the courses of their misfortunes and hope that things turn out positively.

There may be those out there who feel that nature should take its course, thus assuring that only "good" genes are passed on for the benefit of the species, but I just can't agree. This bird is an individual first, a species second. The bottom line is that there are two choices: to let nature take its course, or to intervene. At times hard choices must be made when one encounters these situations, but at other times conditions exist that soften those choices. Fortunately, most people readily agree with the concept that distressed wildlife should be aided. We must be responsible trustees of our natural world and its inhabitants. To me, that means helping when one can. The ability to blend a scientific mind with a compassionate heart allows one to experience the best of both worlds.

It seems that an unprecedented number of rufous hummingbirds appeared in the East in 1993. Apparently two rufous or Allen's type hummers appeared four days before Thanksgiving at the perennial garden of the Wave Hill Conservancy on the Hudson River. These birds either succumbed to the cold the night before Thanksgiving or moved on early Thanksgiving morning; temperatures on Thanksgiving eve were around 15° F., all the flowers in the garden froze, and the birds were not seen again. A different rufous had appeared at a hummingbird feeder in Flushing (Queens County, New York City) in mid-November, and there were four reports for Maryland and one for New Jersey at about the same time. This inordinate number of Northeastern sightings in one season suggests to me that an external force was at play—some common denominator physical in nature, such as a weather or pressure system, and not "bad" genes. Perhaps El Niño was a factor.

Apparently this bird is a species on the move. According to Paul Johnsgard,[1] the rufous has only recently invaded Alaska—so recently, in fact, that flowers adapted for hummingbird pollination have not kept up, and the rufous frequently pollinates flowers more suitable for bees. Many years from now, if we are fortunate enough to still have hummingbirds, those that have been able to expand their ranges will be the ones that survive. The rufous hummingbird is essentially a mountain bird, and the Rocky Mountains mark the eastern edge of its migratory route. Perhaps one day its range may include the mountains of the Eastern states as well.

This is the story of one bird's adventure far from home, and is the chronicle of what will probably be the first confirmed sighting of a rufous hummingbird—a very unusual winter visitor—in New York State. I realize that of all North American hummers, the one most likely to be seen out of its normal range is the rufous. But there has yet to be a confirmed sighting in New York State, and I consider her visit to be an exciting and noteworthy event in the bird world.

Because there was such a sharp, natural division in events, the story is broken into three seasons—autumn,

1. Paul A. Johnsgard, Foundation Professor of Life Sciences at the University of Nebraska at Lincoln, is the author of *The Hummingbirds of North America* (Washington, D.C.: Smithsonian Institution Press, 1983).

winter, and spring—each beginning with a brief syn-
opsis of what Rosie would be doing under normal circumstances and then what she was doing here. Autumn
represents her arrival here and her adjustment period
once she was taken in; winter details her daily routine,
the time that she would ordinarily spend between
migrations, her period of rejuvenation; and spring
describes changes that precede a migration, a wind-
down toward her release.

First and foremost, I have derived great pleasure
and personal satisfaction from being able to offer help
to this bird, as well as from sharing my experience with
others. My greatest hope is that this written account
will contribute in some way to an increased knowledge
of this species.

When I was young, I was told to put butter on a
burn. I didn't listen; I had that "gut feeling" that water
would be better. Likewise, when I was told to take
down my hummingbird feeders by Labor Day, I had
the feeling that the opposite would be better. I know
that the hummingbirds that use the feeders are the first
to leave in the fall, but feeders available later will be a
welcome haven to stragglers while they accumulate
extra weight in preparation for migration. These dar-
ling little stragglers are the bonus birds of the hummingbird season. And this year's straggler was the
biggest bonus of them all.

AUTUMN

Autumn, for our purposes and irrespective of the dates on the calendar, is the time between the end of nesting and the arrival of hummingbirds on their wintering grounds, and consists primarily of the migration.

The rufous hummingbird migrates earlier than is typical for north temperate hummers such as the ruby-throated (*Archilochus colubris*), broad-tailed (*Selasphorus platycercus*), calliope (*Stellula calliope*), and black-chinned (*Archilochus alexandri*). Males tend to precede females, and adults the juveniles. William Calder reports that adult males are first to migrate, arriving at the Rocky

Mountain Biological Laboratory at Gothic, Colorado, as early as the end of June or early July.[2] Females, who follow the southbound males, migrate an average of six days later, and their numbers gradually increase at Gothic until they become more abundant than males. Later, juveniles, making their maiden migrations, start to arrive. The average time between the influx of males and juveniles is two weeks. Transients can usually be found in California through late August.

On the southbound journey, the rufous migrates along one of two major flyways flanking the Great Basin Desert: the Coast Ranges and the crest of the Sierra Nevadas or the Rocky Mountain Cordillera, where they may be found foraging among wildflowers in montane meadows. One such important wildflower is skyrocket, or scarlet gilia (*Ipomopsis [Gilia] aggregata*). The rufous hummingbird is the primary pollinator of skyrocket, which commences flowering by early July, just in time to provide nectar for the migrants. In the early summer, during the beginning of the skyrocket flowering season, broad-tailed hummingbirds, still in their breeding season, and the early migrating rufous hummingbirds descend on large patches of this attractive red flower. The rufous dominates the broadtail on the best territories, which contain not only skyrocket

2. William A. Calder, Ph.D., is professor of evolutionary biology at the University of Arizona at Tucson and the author of "The Rufous Hummingbird," *The Birds of North America*, Life Histories for the 21st Century, no. 53, 1993, and "Migration of Rufous Hummingbirds," *WildBird* 7, no. 5 (May 1993): 43–45.

but penstemon and paintbrushes as well. The adult
male rufous vigorously defends his feeding territory
(temporarily established for southbound refueling)
from both juveniles of his own species and broadtail
competition. Populations remain steady through July,
but by early September all hummingbirds are gone and
the skyrocket begins production of lighter-colored
flowers. The rufous continues south along the central
and southern Rockies and the Sierra Madre Oriental in
eastern Mexico, and then proceeds westward along the
transvolcanic range to its wintering range in Mexico.

An Unusual Visitor

Vagrant birds often stray far from their usual migration routes. Of all the hummingbirds, the rufous (*Selasphorus rufus*) is particularly far-ranging, and particularly so during its fall migration.

I'm not sure just when that hummingbird first appeared in my garden. I do remember, however, that once, while I was trying to take a mental tally of the season's young hummers, I thought, "Oh, yes, and there's that one with the cluster of iridescent gorget feathers that I saw the other day." After I observed a little more of that bird and determined that it was probably a rufous, I began to refer to her as "the little wanderer," which eventually led to "Rosie" from the song "The Wanderer" by Dion.

Perhaps it was the result of El Niño, but 1993's weather was quite the flip-flop from the norm, with West Coast rains ending a drought there that had persisted for several years and many parts of the East experiencing an almost totally rainless summer. The drought was so severe in this part of the Hudson Valley that the average backyard looked more like chaparral than the lush green we ordinarily get in a humid Eastern summer.

That year's weather may also have had an effect on local hummingbirds. Because of the drought, natural food was not plentiful and hummingbirds reportedly flocked to feeders in record numbers. Perhaps more important, albeit less noticeable, with reduced moisture it appears that less insect food was available to feed the young, resulting in fewer subsequent nestings. The number of hummingbirds dropped sharply in early September. Individual birds departed daily, and by the first day of autumn, only three or four hummingbirds could be counted. Because my garden is planned around hummingbirds, there are always birds here late in the season. Until none have been seen for several weeks, the feeders are cleaned and refilled every other day. Because of the garden's attractiveness to hummingbirds, even after the usual residents leave, new birds stop by for a few days to fatten up for their southward migrations, so it's not unusual to have new birds here as late as early to mid-October.

On September 22 I heard a new hummingbird at a feeder just outside the kitchen window. This new bird was very vocal, very loud, and its voice was particularly chirpy. I made a mental note of the obvious *chip-chip-chip*, but each time I attempted to peek at the bird through the window, it would fly off. When I did finally get a glimpse of the new hummer, something else struck me as different: it didn't appear to be of the same proportions as the other hummers. It was not out of proportion, but different. The head seemed larger in relation to the body, and the body shorter and more tapered than usual—a stockier bird. But then I detected what might be the start of a gorget in a loose, horse-shoe-shaped cluster, smack dab in the middle of the throat. This immediately reminded me of a *Selasphorus* species, but that would be virtually impossible in this area. Still, this bird was different and I wanted to get a better look.

Fortunately, after three or four days of only a glimpse here and there, I managed to get that better look. What I saw was exciting. This bird, with a somewhat different green coloring than the rubythroat and with different light green iridescent spotting at the sides of the throat, also displayed a remarkable amount of rufous coloration on the sides, flanks, and tail. That was the coup de grâce—I had to get close to that bird. It might easily have gone unnoticed as just another greenish hummingbird, but now every glimpse I was able to get revealed a little something different. This was not an ordinary rubythroat migrant; this, I was sure, was a rufous hummingbird many, many miles east of its usual migratory route.

I sat hidden in the garden, with field glasses in hand, to observe the bird without frightening it. To my surprise and excitement I could tell that the new hummer was a vagrant member of the genus *Selasphorus*. Although the females and immatures of rufous and Allen's hummingbirds are extremely similar in appearance, I eliminated Allen's (*Selasphorus sasin*) for the most obvious reason—geographic distribution and migratory habits. I was unsure, however, whether I was looking at an adult female rufous or an immature. It certainly looked like a female, but since immatures with no prior migratory experience to draw from are the usual wan-

The tail is the most reliable feature by which to distinguish female rufous from Allen's hummingbird.

derers, I reasoned that this probably was an immature rufous. This was important and exciting. I would have to get photographs and turn them over to someone more qualified than I for a positive identification.

The preeminent authority on the rufous hummingbird is Dr. William A. Calder, professor of evolutionary biology at the University of Arizona at Tucson. He agreed to examine my photographic material and give his opinion. A couple of days later, he called with the news. What I had was indeed *Selasphorus rufus* and the bird was a young adult female. That determination was based on the following: (1) the white tail spots of typical width for a female; (2) no streaking radiating from the chin, which is present on immatures—this bird had a clear throat, indicating an adult female; (3) under a hand lens, the bill appeared smooth, with no ridges or wrinkles common to an immature's bill; and (4) only a few red feathers on the throat (the number increases with age).

The photos also revealed that the bird had molted or otherwise lost two wing feathers. But additional photos—far superior to those I sent to Dr. Calder—were taken one week later and showed even more. The bird was in an active state of replacing the feathers on both wings and new growth was visible. There is a difference in the rectrices, or tail feathers, between the female rufous and Allen's. In the female rufous, the outer rectrices are wider than the female Allen's. The new photos clearly showed the tail to be that of the rufous. This positive identification, documented by photographs, should make this the first confirmed and unquestioned record for *Selasphorus rufus* in New York State.

There have been other Eastern reports for the rufous and several sightings in southern states, including wintering over, but no confirmed record for New York State. While there have been some prior recorded sightings in New York, no photographs were taken and none of these sightings as of this date have been accepted, although a report of a *Selasphorus* species has been accepted.

According to one expert on recorded sightings of birds in New York State, in twenty years there has been one report of a rufous, but within the last fourteen months, there have been three. However promising this may sound, the sightings may reflect the results of a six-year drought in the West. Or they may be due to the increased popularity of hummingbirds, with more people noticing them. Being a typical birder, each time I read of a Western species sighted east of the Rockies, I fantasize about it happening in my yard, though the chances of one of these off-course migrants finding my spot is hardly imaginable. The realization that it did is utterly astonishing.

That the bird was attracted to my yard is no surprise. The large number of other hummers and the many feeders undoubtedly would have gotten its attention, but surely the abundance of flowers clinched the attraction. But what in the world would take this bird so far off its course in the first place? The rufous is the champion migrant of the hummingbird world, making a 2,000-plus-mile trip from its wintering grounds primarily in western Mexico to breeding grounds in western North America from southeastern Alaska and southern Yukon, as far north as 61° N., south to the western Canadian Provinces and northwestern United States. It has an oval migratory route, with its spring movement northward up the Pacific Coast over a variety of habitats at lower elevations and its fall southward trip at

higher elevations via the two major flyways that flank
the Great Basin, and follow the Sierra Nevada and
Coast Ranges or the Rocky Mountains. Because of its
oval migratory route—as opposed to a retracing, or
backtracking of prior steps—there is a natural ten-
dency to move eastward for the southbound journey.
By mid- to late September, female and immature rufous
hummingbirds can be found in Arizona and New Mexico; in Texas, migratory rufous hummingbirds are present from July until late September, with a few
persisting into October.

Recaptures of banded rufous hummingbirds sug-
gest that there is loyalty to the wintering grounds and
the successful migratory routes to reach them. As an
adult, my visiting rufous obviously had at least one successful migration, so why would she be so wrong now?
Storms might throw a migrant off course, the prevail-
ing westerlies could have helped carry it, and recent
magnetic storms on the sun might have interfered with
the bird's ability to navigate. The old string-on-the-
globe trick showed me that the distance from southeastern Alaska to my area is about the same as to a
normal wintering ground. While some say that these
errant migrants can right their mistakes in subsequent
journeys, others feel that the birds will maintain some
alternative form of north-south migration, perhaps
faithfully traveling up and down the East Coast. Perhaps she's made this trip before?

The rufous spent the entire day in the yard except
to sleep, and I do not know where that was. However,

she retired earlier in the evening and arrived later in the morning in relation to available light than did the rubythroats. In Dr. Calder's superb treatment of the rufous for *The Birds of North America,* a copy of which he very kindly provided, he points out that, when on the wintering ground, the rufous's average use of an 11.4-hour solar day is 10.5 to 10.9 hours. This is consistent with the daylight activity I observed.

Somewhat fickle about her choice of feeder, Rosie first used the Perky four-flower type at the kitchen window exclusively (out of sight from those used by the rubythroats). Then, as the rubythroats departed, she branched out and tried them all. Of all the feeder types, however, the small Perky bottle with the tube and bee guard seemed her favorite. Feeding was at intervals of fifteen to twenty minutes, with no increase in frequency at the beginning or end of day, also unlike the rubythroat.

Before and after each feeding, she spent approximately one minute at her perch loudly announcing her presence—*chip-chip-chip.* A very limited amount of time was spent foraging at the flowers. Of the available flowers, she visited the salvia, skyrocket, four o'clocks, honeysuckle, fuchsias, and jewelweed. According to the DesGranges studies, nectar production is best under hot and sunny conditions.[3] Perhaps the feeders are just plain convenient, but since our weather

3. Jean-Luc DesGranges, and P. R. Grant, "Organization of a Tropical Nectar Feeding Bird Guild in a Variable Environment," *Living Bird* 17:199–236.

changed abruptly from hot and sunny to cool and damp, the lack of foraging may well have meant that available natural nectar was insufficient to make hovering in front of the flowers worthwhile.

During the few times I've had the opportunity to observe rufous hummingbirds under natural conditions, I've been struck by how much more pugnacious they are than the rubythroat. They are reported to be the most aggressive of North American hummingbirds, defending their feeding territories during migration as well as on the breeding ground. However, I did not observe any belligerence on the part of this rufous toward the resident or transient rubythroats. I have even seen the bird perching three to four feet away from and in full view of a juvenile rubythroat on one of the bare, arching branches at the top of the weeping cherry tree. The rubythroat was preparing for its migration and had fattened up, but the rufous, obviously already in migration and in spite of the need for extra fat for the southbound journey, showed no such plumpness. The rufous occupies a variety of habitats during its migration, and will spend several days to two weeks at one location before continuing on. Dr. Calder indicated that the expected daily weight gain in a pre-migratory (or, I would presume, refueling) rufous is .25 to .50 gram. This may seem negligible, but relative to the whole, it is significant; it's a gain of as much as 72 percent. Thus for a 3.5-gram bird, when all reserves have been depleted, it can take from five to ten days to be ready to resume a journey.

In comparing species, scientists measure intelligence by relative resourcefulness, proficiency or the ability to adapt. It is evident that hummingbirds are quite intelligent, particularly when you consider the size of the brain, but it may also be that certain species are smarter than others. I do not know where the rufous fits in relative intelligence among hummingbirds, but I was very impressed by my hummer's ability to master the different feeders in an extremely short time—noticeably faster than the rubythroat.

The rufous hummingbird's stay here filled me with many questions. In particular, her behavior toward the rubythroats seemed atypical for the species; perhaps her body was telling her that she was on her wintering ground, where her status is only of intermediate dominance. Might there be something in the genetic makeup that tells a bird how far to go during its migration, or when to stop? If so, she would reach a point when her physiological need to put on weight would cease. Only time would tell.

The Decision

After those first pictures, I had hoped that the rufous hummingbird would stay long enough for me to get some better photos—at least until the next weekend, when I would be able to take my camera outside again. The first thing I did upon returning home from work each afternoon was to check whether Rosie was still there. When Saturday arrived and Rosie was there, I became determined to get shots good enough to unquestionably distinguish her from a female Allen's. After that weekend, I continued to check each day when I arrived home, half hoping for her own good that Rosie would have taken off for warmer parts, but knowing also that I would be disappointed and undoubtedly worried not to see her there. She always was there.

Eventually I became concerned about Rosie. She had made no obvious weight gain and seemed to show no inclination to leave. She had settled in and developed a routine centered in this new territory that she was apparently considering her winter home. I felt sorry for her, so far away from home, all alone and with such an uncertain future.

Each day more summer birds disappeared to be replaced by winter birds. The yellows, golds, oranges, and reds of autumn were all around me and I knew that by Halloween the leaves would have fallen. The mornings were frosty and the nights were getting colder, and less food was available for her foraging. In spite of drastic overnight changes, Rosie appeared at the feeders at the same time each morning, even when temperatures were in the twenties. The rufous is probably a hardier hummingbird than is the ruby-throat; but it wasn't only the cold that concerned me. According to DesGranges, optimum nectar production is achieved at warm temperatures under sunny skies. While his may have been a study under conditions in Mexico, I could relate the information to this area, since hummingbirds here appear to do less foraging under cool and wet conditions, sticking at these times to feeders and catching more insects. Even if and when the flowers are available, frost is not only a genuine threat but nectar stores may be naturally low. The sugar solution in the feeders would continue to give Rosie energy, but what about protein? As she began restricting herself more or less to the feeders, it was obvious that her diet would suffer. And what about the feeders? Could I reasonably expect to keep them from freezing all winter? Life or death for Rosie was entirely in the hands of the weather, and we were on borrowed time.

This area's climate, as that of most of the Northeast, is one of cold, frequently wet winters with ice,
snow, and bitterly cold temperatures often accompanied by strong winds, interspersed with occasional
milder spells (the "January thaw"). Severe weather can
and frequently does endure for days and sometimes
weeks on end. I thought about the March 1993 bliz-
zard, which had dropped seventeen inches of snow on
our area. And I thought about other winter sightings, in
particular a letter to the editor that appeared in the
October 1990 issue of *WildBird* magazine.[4] The writer
related the problems in keeping feeders from freezing
during an out-of-season visit by a rufous in Tennessee
around Thanksgiving, presumably 1989. The area had
experienced a cold wave around mid-December, with
temperatures dropping to below zero most nights until
late December. For several days, the feeders were
changed every twenty to thirty minutes so that the
nectar would not freeze. Eventually a heat lamp was
installed to help keep the nectar liquid. At that point,
the rufous stayed all day near the feeder. The writer
speculated that the bird ultimately succumbed to the
sustained cold. I also thought about a conversation I
had with Jack from The Nature Conservancy's Ramsey
Canyon in southeast Arizona. We discussed two blue-
throated hummingbirds (*Lampornis clemenciae*), who a few
years back were still at the preserve in mid-January.
After an overnight temperature drop to about 14° F.,

4. *WildBird* 4, no.10 (October 1990): 3.

Jack found that one of the birds had succumbed to the cold. Here, we consider it a relatively mild winter if nighttime temperatures don't go below 14°.

Who really knows just how many of these out-of-season wanderers die because they have strayed too far, often on their maiden migrations. A hummingbird is able to withstand subfreezing temperatures for a few days, and may even enter a state of torpor for extended periods, but sustained cold as we experience here is a different story altogether. If I had taken all the feeders down, would that have caused her to leave? I doubt it. There were still flowers around—the same flowers that may have attracted her in the first place. Eventually the flowers would not have been enough to nourish her, and she would have perished from starvation or succumbed to the cold, as the Tennessee bird had. Even if there were no flowers, removing the feeders is the most inappropriate alternative and would have invited a certain agonizing death by starvation.

I recently had a call from a woman in Chicago. She told me of a juvenile male rufous that appeared in her garden last November and remained. As the bird stayed longer, the woman became more alarmed and began telephoning zoos and other organizations for advice on how to handle the situation. Unfortunately, she was ill-advised to take down her feeders to force the bird to migrate, because the bird had already migrated to her yard and had no plans to move on. For the next three days, the bird remained, sans feeders. The woman and her husband then decided to go against the advice, but by that time the bird had succumbed, having exhausted his energy reserves.

So many thoughts passed through my mind. One might expect to see them during July or August, but late September? And what about shelter for Rosie? How much good would an incandescent lamp do? Would she sleep near it? What is a safe drop in temperature? There has to be a point beyond which she could not emerge from torpor.

I worried about when the icy winter winds would cut right through this area, situated at 42° N. To be on the safe side, I dug up a plant of *Salvia coccinea*—just in case everything else was killed off by a hard frost. In a pot and protected in the garage, I would have no trouble finding something to offer her once all the other perennials had turned black. I decided to play it by ear. I would give Rosie every opportunity before I would take action. Each weekend I listened to the extended forecast, thinking, "Well, she can make it through this week. If she's still here next weekend, I'll lure her in." I thought again about the struggle of the Tennessee rufous and the bluethroats at Ramsey Canyon. The thought of finding that frozen little body is a sad one and I didn't want it to happen here. I knew what had to be done.

The night before Christmas was cold and snowy. Christmas Day never made it above freezing, with a little more snow and no sun. The day after it was cold—10° F. in the morning and never out of the teens for the rest of the day. And it was extremely windy—so cold and windy that even all bundled up, I could not be outdoors for the ten minutes it takes to feed the birds. That night went below zero. We were only a couple of days into winter, with the worst yet to come.

There's no need to give a blow-by-blow description of the entire winter—suffice it to say that the first week of January saw snow and bitter cold on six days out of seven, and snow, ice, or freezing rain on almost half the other days in the month—some with a wind chill factor of 40 to 50° below zero. Day after day of 10 to 15° F. below zero at night and only 10 to 15° F. above during the day. January temperatures were below normal (one early-morning temperature was $-24°$ F., the coldest since the 1970s) while precipitation was above normal. In fact, January 1994 turned out to be the coldest, most brutal one on record. I couldn't help wondering about other hummers sighted in the Northeast late in the season. When I looked at the clouds of snow ferociously blowing across the open and now barren backyard, I knew that I had made not only the right but the only choice.

Bringing Her In

Rosie obviously wasn't planning to travel any farther than she had. For the most part, once the competition had departed, the loud *chip-chip-chip* that announced her claim to this territory stopped as well. In her mind she was where she belonged. One night in early October, the majority of flowers were frosted. There was a complete change in the outdoor picture, with a drastic reduction in available nectar. Providing for her outdoors would become increasingly difficult and ultimately impossible. She couldn't possibly make it through winter, irrespective of help. However hardy she might otherwise be, she was just ill-equipped for the rigors of a Northeast winter.

I had a suitable area to offer Rosie and had successfully housed a hummingbird before, so I was less scared this time around. The sunroom had proven itself to be an excellent hummingbird haven for a lengthy stay. Flowers grow there all winter. Squeak had spent a very nonfrustrating several months in that sunroom, relaxed and content, while he reached maturity in preparation for his release the following spring. Rosie had been given every opportunity to continue her migration; as long as there was a chance, no matter how remote, that she might depart on her own, I waited. But she had passed the point of no return. As November approached, I decided to bring her in. I gathered my thoughts, carefully weighing the options. I needed a plan. Rosie was different from the other hummers. She was a skittish bird and she would have to be coaxed. I didn't want to do anything that had the potential of hurting her, so nets were out. I would have to arrange for there to be no other alternative.

Rosie's favorite place in the garden was the circle, an area where sun-loving hummingbird flowers grow in abundance. It is the highest and driest spot in the yard, and the southern half receives sun all day long. In the center of the circle is an overgrown privet with many branches and twigs, and hundreds of places for little hummingbirds to hide. On the shady, north side of the privet, four o'clocks and *Saponaria* flourish, while on its south, tall red cannas form a background for such fall favorites as *Salvia coccinea, Zauschneria californica,* and stands of *Ipomopsis rubra*.

Among the flowers is a tall branch stuck in a pipe in the ground, a place where the hummingbirds may rest, and a NektarPlus feeder filled with sugar-water. Rosie spent much time there, but it was just too far away from the house. She was totally out of reach; I'd have to get her closer. I'd have to narrow down the number of places to visit and draw her closer to the door of the sunroom by creating more abundance where I wanted her to be. I could do nothing—nor would I—about the flowers. I'd have to work strictly with the feeders. The first thing I did was remove some feeders. The next thing I did was move the remaining feeders closer to the house. One feeder that she was particularly fond of was the Perky gravity-type bottle under the spruce tree. That feeder remained, as it was the one that drew her closest. Other feeders were hung under the overhang just outside the sunroom, and were moved gradually closer and closer to the door, thus forcing her feeding activity to gravitate more toward the house.

Next, I stood near the Perky feeder under the spruce tree in an effort to force her to use the feeders near the sunroom door. Eventually, she began to use the target feeders. Once she automatically returned to the feeders near the door, I opened it, hoping that she would notice the flowers inside and go in but she didn't. Finally I moved one of the feeders inside, just beyond the door and I waited. Two cold hours later and without any fanfare, she nonchalantly entered the sunroom and I shut the door behind her. That was the start of our winter together.

WINTER

Although small numbers of rufous hummingbirds regularly winter from Texas eastward along the Gulf coast to western Florida, and occasionally to southern and coastal Georgia, its primary wintering area, as for so many other hummingbirds that breed in north temperate regions, is Mexico. Dr. Calder indicates the birds like shrubby, woodland habitats.

In his paper on the co-existence of resident and migrant hummingbirds in an area of western Mexico, DesGranges describes four selected habitats determined by altitude and running from the semi-arid lowlands at sea level to higher and wetter areas. All four habitats experience a dry winter season from November to June, as is typical of western Mexico, with a major flowering period from December to February. DesGranges indicates that the rufous hummingbird inhabits three of the four habitats along this altitudinal gradient.

The arid-thorn forest, found at the lowest elevations, is an open area of thick undergrowth and thorny vines, containing cacti and flowering trees, most of which are leguminous. The forest is deciduous and flowering occurs primarily in the dry season. The rufous arrives in early January, and its status is territorial (early January might indicate that the rufous's arrival may be the first leg of the spring migration).

The rufous is a "traplining" hummingbird on the open, dry forests of tall pines and medium-size oaks on the arid pine-oak habitat; that is, they follow a regular feeding route between patches of flowers, as opposed to a specific territory. In the arid pine-oak habitat at elevations between 4,920 and 8,200 feet, flowers are the most abundant of all four habitats, with *Salvia*, *Leonotis*, *Stachys*, *Calliandra*, and *Lobelia* blooming during the dry season. *Malvaviscus arboreus* and *Fuchsia parviflora* bloom year-round, but peak in the spring and again in autumn.

The rufous arrives in late November on the humid pine-oak habitat at loftier elevations of over 8,200 feet. This habitat has a wetter and denser forest of oaks with mosses. Except for the white-eared hummingbird

(*Hylocharis leucotis*), inhabitants of this cooler area exhibit daily movements in altitude, going uphill between 7:00 and 8:00 A.M. and then back down to the lowlands for the evening. DesGranges indicates that the green violet-ear (*Colibri thalassinus*), broad-tailed (*Selasphorus platycercus*), and rufous hummingbirds concentrate their foraging on blossoms of *Cestrum terminale, Ribes ciliatum, Buddleia cordata,* and *Senecio angulifolius,* as well as garden plants such as *Jacaranda* and *Musa,* and that they all have territories that they reestablish each morning, with the best going to the "aggressive" rufous. It appears that migrant hummingbirds generally have a status of low domination except the rufous.

Winter was Rosie's period of rest and rejuvenation. It consisted of sleeping, visiting flowers, eating, bathing, preening and scratching, and finishing the molt that had started in September or earlier. It was a relatively quiet period with short days.

Night and Day

When you come right down to it, Rosie wouldn't really be doing anything much different indoors than she would be outside, sitting around, eating, bathing. But it seemed such a monumental change for her, from the complete and unequivocal freedom of moving clear across the country to confinement, no matter what size sunroom. I felt very sympathetic. I knew I had done the best thing, but did she? I also knew that there would be some adjustment to the changes thrust upon her, and I was afraid it would be quite a challenge to get her to come around. For me, it wasn't at all difficult to fall back on having a hummingbird guest for the winter.

Squeak was a last-minute addition to the sunroom, but Rosie was anticipated and that allowed for a little advanced planning. So once it became evident that she would be my winter guest, I got the room ready.

Sleep—To start with, Rosie would be needing a place to sleep, something similar to the skinny branch

Squeak had used. I had discarded that branch and now had to find something suitable for Rosie. I settled on a tall branch with many small, skinny twigs, and this became her "tree." Rosie's "tree" was tall enough so that when placed in the pot of *Salvia coccinea* that had been brought in from the garden, it practically reached the ceiling and branched out across the southeast corner of the room. Eventually the tree became the core of the majority of her activity, with particular branches reserved for very definite actions.

Turning off the fluorescents her first night in the sunroom proved to be somewhat of a problem. I wanted them to turn off around 8:00 P.M., but was afraid to have them operate from the timer lest she be flying around and left suddenly in the dark. It seemed that the only answer was to shut them off manually once she settled down. While she was outside, darkness fell gradually and there was ample time for her to settle in during twilight and ready herself to roost for the night. The situation would be different indoors because, while it appears dark inside, light enters from outside, not only from the twilight but from the street light, porch light and, frequently, moonlight as well. Turning off the back porch light made it seem darker inside, thus the outside light became even more obvious. This undoubtedly was confusing Rosie, and she headed toward more light, hovering right up against the window. Then she landed first on the door lite and then on the windowsill, where she kept her little body pressed against the glass. Since there was little I could do about the ambient light, and I would never be able to make it totally dark outside, I'd have to add a little light inside. I decided to use a night light to balance the intensity between inside and outside, creating a dusky atmosphere that seemed to put her at ease and set the pattern for the remainder of her stay.

In order to survive an energy emergency, the rufous, as do other hummingbirds, may enter a state of torpor. During torpidity all processes slow down as a way of conserving energy. Many hummers would not survive were it not for this state of suspended animation. The onset of torpor, at least for the rufous, relates to energy reserves; that is, they pace themselves according to how much reserve remains. Indeed, Rosie's sleep seemed to deepen, with less nocturnal activity as the night wore on.

Rosie found a new and unusual place to sleep, the root of an Aerides *orchid—it is the perfect size for little hummingbird feet.*

Arousal from torpor is fixed to daybreak. With ample food and overnight temperatures set between 56 and 62° F., I did not expect that Rosie would become torpid overnight. Neither Squeak nor Charlie had and, although Rosie generally consumed less toward evening, the rufous seemed to be the naturally hardier

Sleeping among the Cestrum *leaves, Rosie was difficult to find—just a shiny little green object, smaller than the leaf itself.*

of the two species. As a matter of fact, Rosie seemed to be somewhat of a light sleeper. Not only did she occasionally peck at her wings when she gave all other appearances of being asleep, but she even turned around on a couple of occasions.

For the first two weeks Rosie used a different branch each night, probably looking for just the right one. Since one of her feeders was hung from a branch on her tree, I found it difficult to change the feeders in the morning. The tree would move slightly in the pot

At dawn, Rosie's silhouette as she sleeps at the top of the shrimp plant.

and that movement disturbed her. But then, thankfully, Rosie found a new and unusual place to sleep. She settled on a root of an *Aerides* orchid plant. An orchid root is nothing like an ordinary plant root. Most orchids are epi-phytes—that is, they attach themselves to and grow upon something else, usually tree trunks or branches. Consequently the roots, wandering either along the bark of the host tree or branching out into the air, are thick and firm, some pencil-thick, and covered with a white spongy layer of velamin that absorbs water and nutrients. They are the perfect size for little hummingbird feet.

The *Aerides* has several long roots between twenty-four and thirty-six inches that meander through the air under the skylight. Rosie slept on the same root at the same spot each night after that until mid-December.

Then one night Rosie abandoned the root and decided to sleep near the end of one of the branches on the *Cestrum* plant, less than three feet above the floor. I had to wonder what went on in that little mind when all of a sudden she decided to do something different. There was no apparent reason for the sudden change and there was no building up, the way Squeak had done when he "strayed" that one night and slept on another branch instead of the skinny one. She just changed, period, and that was that. Hidden among the *Cestrum* leaves, she was difficult to find, just a shiny little green object no larger—actually smaller— than the leaves themselves. At times she approached a similar-looking branch when ready to retire, but soon realized it was not the right one. She would then fly back and forth across the room a couple of times before landing on the exact spot of the right branch. It's almost as if one of the ways she remembered where to sleep was by repeating her previous steps, or flights, until it "felt right."

Many of the plants offered to Rosie were grown under lights in my basement and brought up to the sunroom once blooming began. One of the shrimp plants (*Beloperone guttata*) began to flower late in February and when the blossoms started opening, I brought it up to the sunroom. At about that time, when Rosie was ready to roost for the evening, she would fly back and forth across the length of the sunroom, flitting from flower to flower, including the blossoms on the shrimp plant. She'd linger only a split second at each one, and then land on one high branch or petiole after another, as though she were looking for another new place to sleep. When the branch or petiole swayed or if her landing wasn't just right, she'd immediately retreat to her regular sleeping branch on the *Cestrum*, sit for a few seconds, then run through the process all over again. Rosie paid particular attention to the uppermost part of the shrimp plant. Evidently something about that plant appealed to her. Finally on March 3, she landed at the top of the plant and stayed longer than she had at other times. She stayed for perhaps an hour before she got up for her final sip. After her nightcap, she returned to the shrimp plant and spent the night in yet another new spot.

All day long, and especially in the morning, Rosie was a live wire, bathing, preening, flitting from flower to flower, hunting, exploring, and flying all over the room, but as the solar day came to a close, Rosie turned quiet and would leave her perch only sporadically for an occasional sip. The interim branch changed when Rosie's sleeping place changed, so she could face the sleeping spot for five or ten minutes before she retired. She seemed to have a sense of timing, an internal clock. However, if she were to see me during those last few minutes before the lights went out, she would leave her sleeping perch and follow me around for a nightcap.

Such was the case for her second night on the shrimp plant. Unfortunately, on that night the lights went out before she could get back to the branch where she wanted to sleep. She attempted to make her way back in the perpetual twilight that had been created for her, but she missed her mark. On the branch where she landed, she had to grasp the little upright twig sideways. I couldn't imagine that she might be comfortable in that position for the night, so I turned the timer manually until the lights went back on, figuring that when she became comfortable, I'd shut them off again. It went well; she returned, and I quietly passed by her and manually turned the lights off. It worked like the proverbial charm—until I knocked one of the tripods over on my way out. That sent her scurrying and I quickly got the lights back on again before she hurt herself. This time she decided to sleep on the old *Cestrum* branch. After that, I saw to it that she had her nightcap in ample time to return to her sleeping perch. It left me wondering again about what went on in her mind and how and why she made the decision to switch. The following night she retired to the shrimp plant as if she had been sleeping there for months.

If I were standing near her branch when she was ready to retire, she would fly back and forth across the room or circle around me. In fact, it became a nightly ritual to fly around my legs when she wanted to go to her branch, or she would fly in large circles until I moved away from the branch where she watned to be. Every once in a while, after her last drink, she'd fly about four feet away and then come back for another sip, repeating that "here and gone" motion five or six times.

Occasionally Rosie would do something similar to head-wagging before retiring to her branch. Head-wagging with the rubythroat seems to be a territorial matter, with only the most aggressive males displaying such behavior. So I was surprised to see that Rosie also engaged in head-wagging. This was not done from the actual roosting place but from the branch where she would sit after her nightcap. Every once in a while she would swiftly "spin" around on her branch, first facing forward and then backward in a semicircle, tracing and retracing the pattern several times before finally retiring once and for all.

Morning Routine—Rosie's mornings were busy but relatively constant. She awakened immediately when the fluorescent lights turned on. But later the timer had to be adjusted to correspond with earlier sunrises. As soon as the sun rose by 6:30, Rosie awakened each morning a minute or two earlier, and by late February, I had to push the timer ahead daily to accommodate her. On February 25, I was in the sunroom before the lights turned on, when all of a sudden, at 6:18, I heard the purr of her wings, hovering next to me. She was looking for the treat feeder that I held. She sipped and then retreated to her branch. Within a minute, the lights turned on and she started her regular morning chirping. By the first day of spring, 5:45 A.M. was Rosie's time to awaken.

When the lights went on, Rosie would open her eyes and just sit there for almost a minute, looking

Rosie sat quietly in the morning until the sun came up.

from side to side. As she sat a bit longer, her tail would pulsate up and down and her tongue would flick in and out; sometimes she'd empty her crop. She would then stretch her wings back twice while stretching her tail to alternate sides. Frequently while she stretched, I could see that she also stretched her claws. She would then fly directly to the feeder for the first sip of the day.

Her behavior after the initial feeding changed from time to time, although it basically consisted of the same variables arranged in different order or for different lengths of time. When she first arrived, she would sit on one of the high branches of the tree and do some minor preening before moving to the lower branches and getting ready to bathe. But later, once she became totally relaxed, she would leisurely stretch, scratch, preen, peck at her wings, clean her bill, do lots of scratching and shaking her wings while repeatedly fanning her tail in and out. After feeding, Rosie would have a morning bath, dry off, and do some preening. Then she would explore, foraging among the various flowers, and peck at the Spanish moss, at roots and stems, and at windows and walls, presumably hunting for insects.

Keeping Beautiful

When the sun streamed down on Rosie from the skylight above, she shimmered and glowed like a bit of
amber. She was a beautiful bird and she was so diligent
about staying that way. Not a day went by that Rosie

A shower substituted quite well for a gentle rain.

didn't fuss over her feathers, and one of her favorite ways was with water. It is a great deal of fun to watch hummingbirds take a shower in the rain. They lift and spread their tails, flutter their wings, and bare their throats to absorb every drop. They are adorable. Of course, when the rain is heavy, hummingbirds are quick to take shelter. Not only do hummingbirds love to shower in the rain but they also take delight in bathing in the puddles that collect on leaves. In fact, they seem to play in the water, splashing, pecking, and chirping.

In captivity, a shower substituted quite well for that gentle rain and the waterfall for that puddle. The waterfall is a three-level structure chiseled out of a large chunk of black lava. The water spills from a top pool and courses down into another pool, a grotto of sorts, then to a lower pool before emptying into a large, plastic tray that the rock sits in, to recirculate.

Sitting at the edge of the grotto.

Flying over to the top pool.

Once in the water, she splashed and chirped.

The waterfall was made for Squeak so he would have
bath water available at all times, but although he developed an interest in its surroundings, he never took
advantage of this source of water. The sound of trick-

ling water is pleasant and soothing, lending a tropical air to the sunroom. For this reason it became a permanent fixture after Squeak left.

Rosie took her first bath in the waterfall her second day here. No checking it out, inspecting beforehand, or testing—she just went to the waterfall as if well versed in the procedure. She hovered in front of the grotto for a second or two, and then sat on its edge and proceeded to bathe. When she visited the waterfall for a bath, she would spread her tail, splash water by fluttering her wings, chirp, and peck at the water. She stayed four or five seconds, retreated to the *Aerides* root, and then repeated the procedure. She might be in the middle of preening or just sitting there, facing the other way and then she would spin around and make a beeline to the waterfall just as though she had been thinking about it. She did not confine herself to bathing in the mornings; even on snowy, dismal days in March, I watched her go to the waterfall and take prolonged baths late in the afternoon.

In early April, Rosie flew past the waterfall and deliberately skimmed her undersides across the top pool. The next day she sat on its edge. By and by she discovered that the upper level was a delightful alternative to the grotto, and she would fly over and sit right in the one-half-inch-deep pool, fluttering her wings and splashing around to get wet. Frequently she would stop at the edge first and peck at the water a couple of times before getting in. Who knows what made her decide when to go to the pool? Four, five, or six times each day she would head to the waterfall, sit on its edge, and flap, chirp, dip, and dunk. It may have helped to dislodge loose feathers, for I would find them floating on the surface while Rosie was molting. If she got a bit of spider web on her feet or her beak was sticky, she'd take a couple of pecks at her feet or run her beak once or twice across a twig, and then immediately go to the waterfall for the easiest cleaning.

When she was finished at the waterfall, Rosie would be soaking wet and need to dry off. She looked comical, trying to shake out her wings while flying from one perch to another. To dry her wings, Rosie would run her beak across alternating sides two or three times each and then "ruffle" them by taking off from her perch but simultaneously clasping it with her feet so she didn't go anywhere. At times she would spin her wings so fast they became just a blur. Other times she'd just shake them out.

I had a distinct advantage this time around. I knew what Rosie should like and what to expect from her. I felt like an old hand at this hummingbird thing. After allowing her the first couple of days to adjust a bit, it was time to introduce Rosie to the delights of a shower. I started by allowing a very gentle mist to fall over her while she was sitting on one of the lower branches of her tree. She instinctively fluttered her wings. I sprayed again, this time allowing a bit more lukewarm water to reach her. She fluttered her wings again. As I sprayed some more, she pulled her head back and fanned her tail. Her pleasure was evident. After the first shower

Rosie braces herself with her tail during a shower on the Cestrum *leaves.*

she knew what to expect, and within a matter of days, she made the association between seeing the spray bottle and a shower. Indeed, the spray bottle made an annoying noise when I squeezed the trigger; when Rosie heard that noise, she would fly to the shower branch and flutter her wings in anxious anticipation.

Hummingbirds don't play, but Rosie almost seemed to make a game of the shower. On some days she'd chirp while practically jumping from branch to branch, perhaps peck at a couple of drops, hop away to a different branch, come back for another spray, and chirp, chirp, chirp as she repeated all of this over and over. The routine was that I would approach with the spray

bottle and she would go to the shower branch and flutter her wings or squirm around on the leaf. After one or
two sprays, she'd move to a dry branch. I'd spray in the
vicinity of where she had been and she'd come back,
repeating this until she decided that she had played
long enough and then it would be solid spraying. And I
would continue to spray until she was finished. I easily
emptied half the spray bottle of water during each session. One morning I emptied the entire 32-ounce bottle and she still wasn't satisfied. When I returned from
the kitchen with a refill, Rosie was sloshing around on
a wet leaf. Howling winds and the frigid weather of
winter made no difference to Rosie. She got all the
pleasure from her morning shower that she would have
had it been a hot day in July.

During her shower, Rosie would flutter her wings
and spin around, then, with her wings back and arched
up over her back and her tail lifted and spread, she
would turn her head from side to side and chirp. Then
she would rub her head and beak on the twig. Occasionally, she would turn completely around so I could
spray her back. On one occasion, either as a result of
curiosity or because she wanted to be closer to the
water source, she approached the spray bottle and hovered to the side of the stream of water and then crossed
repeatedly from one side to the other.

Once the shower was over, I faced the task of soaking up the water from the slate floor. Rosie, being very
interested in my activity, would hover above me with
head cocked to the side.

Squeak made such a ritual out of drying off while Rosie would simply shake out her wings, sit under the lights and drip dry. She spent little to no time flying around afterward to dry off. When she was finished shaking out, the wet feather sound led directly to the lights, where she'd sit until dry. After drying off, Rosie would do some minor preening. She would run her wing edge through her beak and then shake out the wings. Whatever she did to one side, she repeated on the other—exactly. Even if she scratched her head twice and pulled her foot once over her bill, she repeated it, action for action on the other side. After her bath, she liked to sit on the branch near a tiny, perpendicular twig for beak cleaning. Shaking out her wings was a major part of each preening session. In a typical session she would peck and poke under her wings, shake the wings, preen her tail on one side, shake, preen the other side, shake, run her foot over beak, shake again, peck and poke here and there and then shake out her wings some more.

Rosie watched with great interest the dripping water from freshly watered orchids. She'd dart right over and attempt to peck at the falling drops and then inspect the leaf where a drop had landed. One day she discovered that a soft leaf from the *Cestrum* plant draped over part of the branch was an even more desirable place to shower because of the additional room. This time when she fanned her tail it was more than just spreading the feathers to get them wet. Now she braced herself to stop from falling off the leaf. She tried to stay put by bracing herself with her tail, but still she slid off. I think she especially liked to bathe on the leaves because she liked having something on which to rub her face.

In the winter, when the sun was low in the sky and its warmth streamed through the windows, Rosie would sit in front of the south windows to absorb the rays. Later, when the sun was higher, she sat on the *Duranta* or on another plant in the well of the skylight. She would stretch, and with tail spread would tilt and stretch her neck, baring it so the skin showed in between her feathers and allowed the sun to warm the skin. She obviously enjoyed sunbathing but didn't engage in that activity as much as Squeak did.

Rosie's Winter Garden

The backbone of Rosie's nourishment was NektarPlus, the water-soluble diet of carbohydrates, vitamins, minerals, and proteins formulated specifically for hummingbirds and sunbirds. Still, Rosie had an instinctive need to forage. Perhaps because she was so far off course and I felt sorry for her, I felt a strong need to provide familiar flowers for Rosie to enjoy.

To start with, Rosie had bright red flowers from the *Salvia coccinea* that I had dug up and brought in. It continued to bloom sporadically during the entire winter and spring, and Rosie enjoyed the flowers whenever they were available. The impatiens was also available throughout her stay. Next were the ever-popular fuchsias, always a hit with the hummers, especially the *Fuchsia triphylla* hybrids. Fuchsias were a standby for Rosie—she visited them regularly—but as we shall later see, they were not her favorite.

The initial impression that one might get of a hummingbird working a flower patch is that they are oppor-

Fuchsia triphylla
*hybrids are especially
attractive to humming-
birds.*

tunists who try everything. While this may be true to
some degree, especially when the birds are young and
learning about the world around them, adult hummers
have learned and show definite preferences. *Salvia coccinea* is a rubythroat favorite, as is bee balm (*Monarda
spp.*), but the hummers will all but ignore the bee balm
in favor of the salvia in almost every instance. Since
most of my flowers are grown with hummingbirds in
mind, I had plenty to offer Rosie—the gorgeous scarlet
bouvardia, or trompetilla (*Bouvardia ternifolia*) of the
Southwest, with its two-inch-long, tubular, scarlet flowers; the monkey flowers (*Mimulus* and *Diplacus spp.* and
hybrids) of the West Coast; fuchsias and shrimp plants
(*Beloperone guttata*), scarlet bush (*Hamelia patens*), and fairy
dusters (*Calliandra spp.*). But I wanted something different for Rosie. I wanted to offer her flowers familiar to
her—rufous preferences. I wanted her to feel at home.
The most logical and easiest solution was to acquire
some West Coast natives that the rufous is known to

work; chuparosa (*Beloperone [Justicia] californica*), currants (*Ribes spp.*), and manzanitas (*Arctostaphylos spp.*) would bloom in winter, others not until spring.

All species of *Ribes* are important to hummingbirds because they provide nectar during winter and early

Inspecting Alstroemeria *flowers.*

spring. Blooming from October to March is the beautiful, pink, chaparral currant (*R. malvaceum*); both pink-flowered currant (*R. sanguineum*) and white-flowered currant (*R. indecorum*) bloom from January to March; fuchsia-flowered gooseberry (*R. speciosum*) blooms from January to May; hillside gooseberry (*R. californicum*) blooms from February to March; golden currant (*R. aureum*) from April to

Ribes malvaceum *was the first of the currants to bloom.*

It was followed by Ribes indecorum.

May; and pink Sierra currant (*R. nevadense*) from April to July. Farther north, where seasons are later, these plants flower somewhat later. I wanted to offer a good variety that would bloom over an extended

By Christmas, Mimulus cardinalis *was in bloom.*

period so *R. malvaceum, R. indecorum, R. nevadense,* and *R. speciosum* were selected.

The West Coast native scarlet monkey flower (*Mimulus cardinalis*) is a perennial that may grow to three feet and will prosper under a variety of conditions from sun to shade, but it loves regular watering. The showy, two-inch scarlet flowers appear most of the year and are important hummingbird flowers in the wild. Squeak loved it and Rosie did, too. By mid-December there was evidence of bud formation and to Rosie's delight, by Christmas the first of the *Mimulus* plants had blossoms. Rosie's fancy for these flowers

was evident by the frequency of her visits; the unmis-
takable yellow *V* stamped on her forehead and crown
revealed her actions. As a matter of fact, I could walk
into the sunroom, look at the pollen on her head, and

New Diplacus
puniceus *began*
flowering in mid-
January.

know exactly where she had been: a fluorescent pale
yellow *V* meant *Mimulus*, yellowish-orange, the honeysuckle, and so on.

Related to *Mimulus* is *Diplacus*. The *D. puniceus* hybrids
that Squeak had relished so began its flowering in mid-
January and offered rather longish, slender, red tubular
flowers. Azalea-flowered diplacus (*Diplacus bifidus*), as its
name suggests, looks a bit like a yellowish-orange aza-
lea. Rosie kept a watchful eye on the first buds as they
matured in the sunroom and checked repeatedly, waiting
for them to open. When they did, she treated the plant
with much less enthusiasm than she had led me to
believe she would.

Visiting Turk's cap.

Chuparosa is a member of the mainly tropical Acanthus family, many species of which are attractive to hummingbirds. The flowers offer winter sustenance to Anna's (*Calypte anna*) and other hummingbirds. It is a difficult plant to grow indoors, as it requires a very arid atmosphere and abundant sun. The plant grew quite well, I thought, but flowering was somewhat sparse. When it did develop some flowers, Rosie was so anxious to get to the nectar that she wouldn't even wait for them to open completely, forcing her beak into unopened buds and ruining most of them. She was obviously familiar with chuparosa and poked around at the buds when they were just beginning to show some color.

Orchids are beautiful flowers. Some are big, bold, and colorful, and some are soft and delicate. All are delightful, but most are passed up by hummingbirds. Species in the genera *Aerangis, Angraecum*, etc., all mem-

bers of the Orchidaceae, hold copious amounts of
nectar in their spurs—some of which are as long as
one foot. Most will recall learning about Darwin, who
theorized that a moth must exist with a proboscis at
least as long as the spur on a certain flower in order to
attract the moth and thus pollinate the flower. The
flower to which he referred is an *Angraecum* orchid. Just
as Squeak had, Rosie loved the *Aerangis rhodosticta* hybrid

Rosie showed only moderate interest in fiery spike.

when it was in flower, as she did other Angracoids. She
would return over and over to the same flower, pushing
her beak in as far as it would go to get the nectar. Her
tongue is essentially as long as her bill, yet her tongue
was not long enough for the length of the spurs on
some of the *Angraecum* and *Aerangis* hybrids. Still, she
managed to get enough to satisfy herself and she came

back again and again almost as if she knew that she hadn't gotten it all. She knew where all the developing orchid buds were and periodically during the day she would visit each one to remove the sweet, viscous liquid that they produce. She also managed to find that same nectar-like substance produced on stems of *Laelia albida* just as Squeak had done. I was delighted to see that she was comfortable enough to explore. Unlike Squeak, however, she continued to visit the *Laelia* flowers after they opened, indicating that there was a supply of nectar accessible to her. Blooming in late November and December and coinciding with the start of the dry season in its native habitat, *L. albida* flowers at elevations of over 6,000 feet, at a time and in areas where rufous hummingbirds may be found

Late winter offered Martha Washington geraniums.

Rosie would find only one flower on a plant—here it is Hamelia cuprea.

wintering over. *Rodriguezia venusta* is a lovely, white, botanical orchid from South America and was her favorite of the orchids. Once discovered, it was never left alone. As a matter of fact, Rosie liked it so much that when I held her feeder about eight inches away from those flowers, she "hemmed and hawed," moving back and forth and turning from side to side, as if trying to decide which to choose.

Members of the Acanthus family, *Ruellia* is a genus of attractive, if not spectacular, brightly colored, funnel-shaped flowers. Most varieties grow in Brazil. Three that are grown here are *Ruellia macrantha*, *R. makoyana*, and *R. graecizans*. *R. macrantha* is a full six feet tall and bears clusters of large, beautiful, deeply textured, rosy-pink trumpet-shaped flowers. Rosie visited the flowers of this striking plant, but definitely preferred the other two small and more suitable *Ruellia*s.

Rosie showed only a passing interest in two important Mexican flowers from the DesGranges list: sleeping hibiscus (*Malvaviscus arboreus*) and the two *Calliandra* species that I grow. Turk's cap (*Malvaviscus arboreus var. drummondii*) is an important hummingbird flower on its native habitat from the southern Edwards Plateau to the Rio Grande Plains and along the Gulf coast from Florida to Mexico. Rosie loved Turk's cap, a smaller, somewhat squat version of sleeping hibiscus, but showed absolutely no interest in its relative. Because *Calliandra* (fairy duster, powder puff) is one of the cited winter flowers on the arid pine-oak habitat, I was anxious for the flowering to start on the two from that genus that grow here. To my surprise, Rosie showed only a limited interest in either of these flowers. Even after trying them, she rarely went back for seconds.

Interaction

In his discussion of hummingbird memory and social behavior, Johnsgard recounts the remarkable story of one Mr. Fitzpatrick and his relationship with a particular rufous hummingbird. Fitzpatrick spent several months watching a rufous that had taken possession of a feeder the man had hung outside his bedroom window at a California sanitarium. When the man eventually ventured outdoors, the hummer greeted him by hovering in front of his eyes and flying about his head. About one year later, when Fitzpatrick returned to his home about eight miles away, the rufous followed him and took up residence near his house. The bird is reported to have accompanied Fitzpatrick on his daily walks, warning him of dangers and calling his attention to animals that Fitzpatrick otherwise might not have seen, and is also reported to have ridden on a piece of rawhide rifle sling. When Fitzpatrick again returned to his home after a one-month absence, he was greeted within moments by the rufous, who again flew around his head and hovered in front of his eyes. The story is the most amazing account of hummingbird and human interaction that I have read yet.

At first Rosie was quite skittish and would fly around in the well of the skylight whenever she saw someone. But that behavior soon subsided, becoming reserved for times when I was right in the room. Before long, Rosie felt confident enough to just leisurely retreat to the opposite side of the room from me and eventually she'd even stay on the same side if I didn't get too close. She relaxed and basically ignored me. It didn't take very long to get her turned around after that, and what made her relax around me the most was receiving a shower. After breaking that barrier, it was time to make friends. I knew that Rosie could overcome any remaining apprehension, and a relationship could develop. But I also knew I'd have to work at it. One can hardly expect a bird that would not even bond with another bird to bond with a human much beyond taking what is given, but I was extremely optimistic. Once the initial adjustment phase passed and she became more relaxed in my presence, we could get down to the business of making friends.

The way to any animal's heart is first to encourage it to feel relaxed around you, best accomplished by quiet behavior, slow and steady movements, and only moderate eye contact initially. Next is to offer it something special and desirable to eat. I wanted to give Rosie the ideal diet that NektarPlus provides, but I had to break the barrier and a sweet treat was the way.

Since I planned to start offering Rosie a treat early in her stay—and I knew that it would be sustained over several months—a 3:1 ratio of water and sugar would be a good minimum starting point. Rosie had a definite curiosity about me that indicated she was ready. The first time she fed from my hand in mid-November, it took at least half an hour of tempting and coaxing, and her effort consisted of darting movements and rapid flicks of the tongue in and out at the feeder tube versus the long, lazy sips when she drank alone at the feeder. She liked it very much. When she made the association between the hand-held feeder and something sweet, and she wanted the feeder that was being held, the ratio was increased to 3.5:1 and finally 4:1, the best ratio. At that point, I felt comfortable about the occasional deviation from her perfect diet. As her confidence in me increased, short sips turned into long drinks and the darting movements gave way to relaxation.

Once that plateau was reached, Rosie became brazen enough to let *me* know when she wanted a treat. Whereas Squeak would follow me about the sunroom and dance around my head, openly soliciting, even insisting, upon a treat, Rosie's approach was to retire to what she had categorized as the spot to be handfed and to excitedly chirp alternating with a flick of her tongue in and out. When she saw me entering the room holding the feeder, she immediately went under the lights and waited.

And that's the way it was for quite some time. Then one day she discovered that I could be elsewhere in the

After taking a sip, she moved backward about two inches and flicked her tongue in and out.

Before Rosie left her branch for a treat, she would stretch her wings, fan her tail, and squeal.

room and still feed her. Once she stopped associating her treat with that one particular spot and associated it instead with me, she changed her behavior and would hover inches away from my face, waiting. As she really settled in, she redesigned the scenario and the south-east corner became her headquarters. She then pre-ferred that everything emanate from that area, including being handfed. I knew she really trusted me when she would hover inches away from the hand that held the treat feeder and look out the window with her back to my hands! Each time I'd handfeed her, I'd say, "sip, sip."

Eventually it reached the point where if I said those words, she'd dash to where I was standing. After taking a sip she would move back about two inches, flick her tongue in and out five or six times so just the tip showed, chirp, and then come back for another sip. She would then retire to a branch and chirp—not the loud *chip-chip-chip*, but a soft and sometimes very soft chirp. Once she felt comfortable around me she seemed to take particular delight in flying right up to my face and then whizzing by my head, only centimeters away.

In many ways, Rosie was a creature of habit, desig-nating certain places for specific activities. In the begin-ning when she wanted a treat, she would fly over to the *s*-hook under the lights, where I had first gotten her to use a hand-held feeder. Later when she wanted some-thing, Rosie would charge at me. She'd sail right across the room so quickly that she could barely be seen mov-ing and then she would hang there in midair in front of my face, just looking at me with her tail fanned and slightly curved, appearing completely motionless except for her wings and flicking tongue. If I didn't respond, she chirped—always louder than usual.

When truly relaxed, Rosie settled down snugly on top of her feet.

Likewise, when she was ready for her shower, she'd alight on the "shower branch" of her tree and shake her wings out, perhaps peck at them a bit, and chirp, going through the motions she associated with what she wanted in order to get the idea across. She was communicating with me. Most often, when I would call her, she'd turn her head and look at me. If I were holding the feeder, she'd come over immediately. Each time I would imitate the soft *t-chip* noise she made after drinking, she'd lift her wings a tad as if she were planning to fly off.

Rosie had taken to following me around. One day

she daringly followed me into the potting closet, a four-by-six-foot area with sliding louvre doors off the sunroom. She stayed, hovering, for only a second or two and then departed. She is just a little humming-bird, no different in many respects from any other hummingbird, but she had become very special to me.

She'd fly right up to my face, emit one chirp, and leave.

Rosie accepted my presence very nicely and as time went on, she seemed to enjoy having me nearby—and even developed a curiosity about everything I did. When I talked softly to her she would shake out her wings while sitting, looking at me, just as she did when having a shower. When I sang softly to her, she would cock her head and listen to me. At these times she seemed partic-ularly relaxed. When Rosie would settle down snugly on top of her feet and become puffed up and flat-looking at her bottom, she was the epitome of relaxation.

I really wanted her to sit on my finger. One ruby-throat who had spent an October day with me in 1987 during an early freak snow and ice storm needed only to be nudged to move to my finger to sit and preen; she even allowed me to walk around with her on my finger. Oh, how I wanted to hold Rosie. I knew I could have just gone over and scooped her up from behind while she was on her sleeping branch, but I couldn't bring myself to betray her confidence in me. It would have to be done in a straightforward manner or not at all. Sometimes, particularly when I would talk to her, she'd fly right up to my face, two or three inches away, emit one chirp and go back to her branch. I'm not sure if that was positive or negative, but it's the same chirp as the one she emitted after drinking.

Eventually Rosie became brazen and feisty enough that, if I were doing something with the plants in a place where she wanted to be, she would hover above my head and, in effect, holler at me until I departed.

Rosie liked a nightcap and was given her very last drink of the evening while she sat at her sleeping spot, but prior to retiring she would fly over to the tree to wait for a treat, shoot across the room the minute she saw me and then take her very longest drink of the entire day, really fueling up for the night. Most often Rosie kept her feet tucked in while feeding at flowers, but one thing I noticed as she stopped in front of the hand-held feeder was that her feet would go through motions similar to treading water. They seemed to be paddling, alternating one foot in front of the other. I wonder if that helped her stop. For her nightcap, Rosie took very long drinks, pushing her beak almost all the way into the feeder and ingesting so much that she caused a bubble to float up to the top while she was drinking. She would then fan her tail and, keeping the tail spread, move up a little to inspect the bubble to make sure it was no threat to her. For her last sip she would sometimes take one sip; fly five or six feet away, low toward the floor; stop; hang there and look at me for a second or so; and then come right back for more, repeating these actions four or five times.

One evening she took her last sip of the day, after which she proceeded to hover all around my legs about eight to ten inches off the floor, around and around, back and forth. Then I realized what else she wanted— I was standing too close to the *Cestrum* branch where she wanted to settle in. As soon as I moved, she positioned herself in her then-regular spot. On other nights she refused to settle in until after I left the room. One afternoon as darkness began to fall, I do believe Rosie was chasing me from her territory. Each time my back was turned she'd fly after me chirping or warning loudly and then, when I'd turn around, she'd fly back and forth and then return to her branch. When I finally left the room, she immediately retired to her sleeping branch. But flying around my legs didn't always signify a desire for her to settle in for the evening. There were other times when she would fearlessly fly around my legs, about one foot above the floor, weaving in and out, hunting bugs.

I wanted to photograph Rosie, not only for this book but for my memories, for I knew one day she'd be gone. But she bordered on being downright and deliberately uncooperative. While I'd spend half an hour sitting, camera and flashes poised and ready she, instead of visiting bougainvillea, for instance, or the waterfall, would inspect the reddish-orange "ready light" on the flashes. Then, if I left the room for a minute, I'd return to find her at the bougainvillea or just leaving the waterfall, soaking wet. While I would stand in position, six inches away from the camera, she would decide that she wanted a treat instead, and would fly back and forth in the five-inch space between my eyes and the viewfinder. On one occasion as I sat poised and ready to get some shots at the waterfall, she decided instead to investigate every red snowflake on the arms of my pajamas. In fact, Rosie investigated me any time she felt something warranted inspection—a solid red dot that was part of the logo on a t-shirt, my lipstick, a colorful hairpiece. Eventually the tripods became something to fly around, or under, when she had someplace to go. Rosie immediately investigated everything in her room; therefore, the best picture-taking opportunities came just after a flowering plant was brought in.

I've read that it's the feeders hummingbirds recognize, not the people, but I do not believe this to be so in Rosie's case. One day my husband asked if he could come in to handfeed her a treat. She came over to the feeder immediately but she was reluctant to drink. She knew the person was different. And it was more than just *seeing* the feeder. One early March morning the light of dawn brightened the sunroom just before the fluorescents turned on. Rosie sat with her back to me. I said, "Good morning, Rosie," and she immediately turned around and came over to the feeder without going through her stretching routine. So it's obvious that she both recognized me as an individual and associated at least my voice with a treat. Association is apparently more than just visual. When she heard that annoying, raspy squeak of the spray bottle, she immediately went to her shower branch. When I called her name, followed by the words, "sip, sip," she immediately came over to look in my hand for the feeder. To test her, I frequently did this with my back turned. The stimulus was the sound.

She clearly knows the difference between people—at least between me and others. When my daughter came in to help with some photos of Rosie being handfed, Rosie investigated her over and over, flying right up to her face, approaching from both sides of the camera, from under the camera, in between the legs of the tripod, from behind Terry's head. She knew that this was not me.

And she knew where I kept the feeder. She would shoot over there and hang in midair, waiting for me to turn around and pick it up. When she saw me moving the feeder, she'd move that foot or two to meet it. She understood that I had to go to that spot to pick up the feeder before I could give her some. At times Rosie couldn't decide whether she wanted a flower or the feeder so, on her way over for the treat, would take a poke at a flower or two. At times I wondered if she knew what she wanted at all. She'd go to the shower branch and flutter as if to say, "I want a shower," then she'd fly right up to my face and hover there with tail fanned, chirping as if to say, "I want a treat." In a whimsical manner, she'd repeat her behavior over and over as though she were playing a game. With the abundance of flowers, there were times when she behaved quite independently, refusing the treat in favor of flowers, especially during the spring when she had so many to choose from. Deep down inside, I knew that was best.

To a creature as small as a hummingbird, the sunroom must seem like a jungle with all of the plants inside but Rosie knew her way around in every nook and cranny, under and between pots, cork bark and other mounts, stems, roots, and branches—she always seemed to know exactly where she was going and the only thing I ever noticed her brush against was my hair.

Plumage

When first hatched, the rufous is about the size of a honeybee and naked except for two slight tracts of grayish natal down along the back. The natal down grows longer each day. Pinfeathers begin to show on the sixth and seventh days, and the chicks are soon feathered in juvenile plumage. The juvenile plumage in both sexes is similar to that of the adult female, with some minor differences such as more streaking at the throat. Except for a metallic greenish-bronze head, and occasionally on the back, the adult male rufous is primarily a noniridescent, cinnamon-rufous bird with a brilliant scarlet gorget. It has the distinction of being the only north temperate hummingbird that has evolved from iridescent to pigmented coloring; there is hardly any mistaking the identity of this bird. And as attractive as the male rufous is, the female is as beautiful. The adult female is an iridescent green to bronzy-green bird with white underparts and rufous coloring at the sides and flanks. Her throat is white, speckled with scarlet red centrally and greenish laterally and her tail flashes rufous.

Hummingbird feathers are both beautiful and efficient, but like everything else, they wear out. Molting is the periodic replacement of those old and worn-out feathers. The process is a gradual one and, at least for most U.S. hummingbirds, occurs primarily in winter. Especially because Calder had indicated that the molting cycle and chronology for the rufous are undescribed, I tried to monitor feather loss and replacement.

For the rufous hummingbird, flight feathers are reportedly replaced in January, with males ahead of

Molt of the contour feathers started at the throat and they were lost in bunches.

females. The entire molting period appears to run normally from mid-December until late March. However, as the initial photographs revealed, Rosie's flight feathers were obviously being replaced at least by the second half of September.

By the first week of November, when Rosie began her stay in the sunroom, she was molting at the edges of her throat. I would find her feathers on leaves when plants were removed to be watered, discover them on the floor, or see them floating in the air. Within a week she had a dark half-moon below the gorget area where feathers had fallen out. The loss was rapid compared to Squeak's. It started at the left side of the throat line and as each group was replaced, the next bunch would fall out, thus working the molt across to the right side of the throat.

Rosie lost contour feathers in bunches. What I didn't realize is that occasionally a cluster of feathers falls out together. On December 4, one bunch of eight

Rosie scratched constantly.

The number of iridescent gorget feathers increased from a loose horseshoe shape to a striking central patch.

to ten feathers fell out or were scratched out at once, stuck together at the tips of the quills. Loose feathers obviously annoyed Rosie and probably made her feel itchy. She scratched constantly, frequently in midair, and took more baths per day, with several visits to the waterfall. Rosie would scratch and then shake to dislodge loose feathers, watching them as they softly and slowly floated down to the floor. Occasionally she would meet one halfway down to inspect it. The iridescent contour feathers started to molt in mid-December.

Just as Dr. Calder had suggested, the number of iridescent feathers in the gorget area increased and what had previously been a loose horseshoe became a striking central patch of iridescence as, by late December, new iridescent scarlet feathers formed in a cluster on

her throat. By January 1, pinfeather sheaths were show-
ing above her right eye and on her forehead. On January 4, feather replacement was taking place under her
tail at the side as well as over her head and dorsal areas.
On January 8, pinfeather sheaths were visible on her
forehead; by January 10, they were visible under her
right wing and lesser underwing coverts; and on January 15, pinfeather sheaths were visible on the breast
and abdomen.

Through December 31, 110 contour feathers were
found, including the cluster. Of that total, twenty or 18
percent had iridescent tips. In the two-week period of
January 1 through January 14, forty-eight feathers were
found, 50 percent of which showed some iridescence.
In the next two-week period, January 14 through January 31, twenty-seven contour feathers were found, all
of which showed either iridescence or rufous coloration. In the month of February, two contour feathers
were found, one with and one without iridescence, and
in March only one plain feather was found (March 3).

Although 188 contour feathers were found, many
had not been replaced. Replacement of Rosie's contour
feathers was concurrent with flight feathers, took
place over the entire length of flight-feather replacement, and were lost in a pattern. The pattern seems to
be that feathers were lost at intervals of about seven
days, were lost for two or three days in a row and then
none were lost for about four or five days. There was a
cycle of approximately one week for feather loss, rest,
and replacement.

I can relate only what I actually found, and although I made a diligent effort to find them all, they are all very small and many undoubtedly found their way into inaccessible places. Because of their larger size and small number, primaries were easiest to monitor. The pattern was from the base to tip of the wing except that the ninth primary was skipped, the tenth was molted after the eighth, and then the ninth after the tenth. On November 24 and November 25, Rosie lost the sixth primary on each side. One was found on the floor, the other in the waterfall. Then on December 18, approximately three weeks later, Rosie was acting as though she were extremely agitated, fluffing and shaking her wings and tail, and chirping, loudly and incessantly. The next thing I knew, the seventh primary was lying on the floor beneath her. A search of the surrounding area found its counterpart, which would have had to have fallen out that day or the one before.

On December 23, Rosie's behavior was again very agitated. She hovered around three times in a small counterclockwise circle no larger than four inches in diameter and sat back down. Then, as she lifted from her branch, the eighth primary, left side, fell out. She then proceeded to peck at her left wing repeatedly in the same spot. The next day Rosie came over for a treat when all of a sudden she buzzed and returned to her branch as the eighth primary, right side, fell out. On December 26, Rosie was flying back and forth, again in an agitated manner, and sounding much like a sputtering motor—I could see a dark area on the usu-

Replacement of Rosie's contour feathers was concurrent with flight feathers—as Rosie visits Ribes malvaceum, *different areas of molt are obvious.*

Molting and replacing flight feathers.

ally transparent wing, where one feather overlapped another as it made its way forward; this, too, must have been uncomfortable.

Molting and replacing flight feathers.

Several areas of molt.

By the end of the month, the sound had returned to much more of a soft purr, but on December 30, the soft purr of the morning turned dull by 5:00 P.M. I could hear the difference in the wing sound immediately, and when I searched, I found the slightly curved and thinner tenth primary from both the right and left wing. Finally, on January 8, Rosie held her right wing straight out and was pecking at it when she suddenly got up and flew in one three-foot-diameter circle, counterclockwise, and the ninth primary fell out. The tip was worn. Then, within half an hour while she was hunting, the ninth primary on the opposite side fell out. The tip was unworn. As far as primaries one to five are concerned, I am assuming that they were replaced during the six-week period she spent in the garden before moving into the sunroom.

By January 15, the new tenth primaries were visible. On January 22, the ninth primaries started coming in while pinfeather sheaths for the tenth were still visible and the tenth was about 75 percent complete. The white pinfeather sheaths stood out even while Rosie was hovering, but by January 29 they were gone and her wings sounded normal.

In his paper, Calder indicates that at times rectrices number three to five (the outer three) are not molted by the female, who arrives on her breeding ground with color-marked or worn outer tail feathers. Rosie apparently had started her molt at least in September, by the end of January had stopped and much had been replaced with the exception of her entire tail. Every once in a while she'd hover and vibrate her tail as if she were trying to get rid of something—maybe one of the tail feathers. The noise was loud, but the feathers stayed in. There were times when she'd sit and rattle her tail feathers as if trying to dislodge one, but it was a fruitless attempt as the feathers remained intact.

SPRING

Rufous hummingbirds start their northward spring migration very early in the year, with some departing their winter haunts as early as January. Much of their year is spent traveling. Although stragglers may still be found on the wintering grounds in Mexico, some individuals arrive as early as late February to their breeding areas in the state of Washington. With males preceding females, the bulk of the migrants move through central California in April, for an ultimate mid-April to early May arrival in the Pacific Northwest and southern Alaska, where they inhabit forest openings and brushy places.

Quite simply, the rufous hummingbird has an elliptical migratory route more or less around the deserts: up the coast in spring and down the Western mountains in fall. The pattern coincides with advantageous weather conditions and the onset of blooming of such preferred species as the tubular red to yellow flowers of chuparosa, which is native to semi-arid areas of California, Arizona, and New Mexico; the many species of currant that flower in succession from fall to spring; as well as ocotillo, salvia, penstemon, and delphinium.

One has only to look at the fundamental nature of the West Coast climate to see how a successful migration can take place so early and how the birds can be so far north compared to the Northeast migration. The coast is mild year-round, with a late fall and winter rainy season, and a dry summer. Spring on the West Coast is an early affair. By December, Anna's hummingbirds are beginning to nest in California. By January, the manzanitas are starting to bloom in many areas of coastal California, while lupines, larkspur, paintbrushes, and other wildflowers bloom along roadsides in southern California. By February, fruit trees are in bloom along the coast and up through the Central Valley. Many slopes just south of San Francisco are covered with the blossoms of peaches, apricots, cherries, and nut trees. In contrast, spring in the Northeast lags far behind. In January, when many rufous hummingbirds begin to migrate, we are having snow and cold. In

February, when fruit trees start to bloom on the coast
and hummers begin arriving on their breeding grounds,
we are having more snow and cold. In the sunroom,
however, Rosie flitted around the tropical habitat that
had been provided for her, oblivious to the horrendous
conditions out of doors.

Spring is a time of new beginnings everywhere. The
sunroom was exciting with new buds peeking out on an
entirely different array of plants for Rosie to savor—a
smorgasbord of flowers. It's the time of year when she
should have been on the move, but she wasn't. I felt
badly about being the one who had stopped her, and I
did all I could to make it up to her.

Out of necessity, Rosie would, unfortunately, be off
her normal schedule. But in spite of that, her behavioral
changes appeared consistent with what would have
occurred naturally, had she gone to Mexico, and all her
natural changes occurred in order.

In her annual cycle, winter ended and spring
began with the completion of her molt at the end of
January and, if I may be presumptuous, her natural
increased intake of insects. This would be just prior to
the start of her regular northward migration. The sun
changed and days got longer, only slightly noticeable
in January but the tempo picked up in February. Rosie
exhibited a definite change in behavior, with activities that seemed to parallel normal rufous behavior,
and it all seemed to be falling into place. Her behavior took on more of a skittish aspect, particularly with

others, and she would repeatedly fly to the north side of the room. Whereas January revealed an increase in protein consumption, the desire waned somewhat in February as her "movements" began. By late March, when her movements stopped, Rosie showed an interest in nesting materials.

Spring Behavior

Hunting—Nectar is a rich, renewable resource imparting quick energy, but it is an incomplete food source. The need for protein has been well established, and NektarPlus has proved itself for a well-balanced diet in captivity. Yet there is, apparently, a time or times during the year when protein needs are greater than usual. DesGranges indicates that migrant hummingbirds spend 61 percent of their foraging time before spring departures feeding on insects, as compared to only 1 percent in mid-winter.

For Rosie, insects were a regular supplement to her diet. But birds and animals seem to know what they need and when they need it, and Rosie's desire for insects reached a peak around the start of the year. Too much should probably not be read into this, but it coincides perfectly with completion of the molt and the start of migration, when insects normally form a greater proportion of the total diet. This might be instinctive behavior, and further may coincide with or in some way initiate the start of certain glandular activity that helps the bird get ready for breeding. This very noticeable change indicates that increased consumption of insects occurs, not as a result of increased avail-

The screen of the skylight was an excellent spot for finding little flying insects.

ability or lack of suitable floral nectars, but as a necessary part of the cycle.

One might wonder just what Rosie could possibly do all day. Much time was spent foraging among the flowers, of course, but Rosie would also bathe, sunbathe, preen, just hang around, and hunt. As we got closer to spring, Rosie did more and became more active. At first she spent a small portion of the day hunting. She would visit different places looking for insects, but primarily it was incidental to some other activity. However, around the start of the year I noticed that Rosie was spending much more time hunting. At first I became concerned. But as she began hunting relentlessly, I realized that Rosie just wanted more. She looked everywhere, up and down walls and under leaves. She thoroughly investigated the Spanish moss; every speck of dust, every blemish, and every dried-up raindrop on the window was checked out, too. She captured some insects in midair and plucked others off the windows, leaves, and every other place imaginable. The screen of the skylight was an excellent spot for finding little flying insects.

Rosie was a much more aggressive hunter than Squeak had been and would take off like a little cheetah and, with her mouth open to an angle of approximately 45°, would capture an insect with a snap. One whitefly had the misfortune to land right on her bill. She whipped her head around to dislodge it, opened her mouth wide, and devoured it. I think that the preferred manner of insect collecting is capturing on the fly. When stationary, the insects at times get stuck on the tongue.

Rosie had a different place to sleep, bathe, rest, and hunt. Her favorite hunting branch was a low branch on the *Cestrum*, about one foot above the floor, where she would sit and watch until she spotted something appealing. She would also hover close to the floor, looking for her prey. I really shouldn't say "hover," because that implies that there is no forward movement. This vertical flight was somewhat choppy; she would sputter no more than 2 inches above the floor and check out the entire sunroom for insects, looking under everything. And she would look up and down my legs, during which time I was afraid to move lest I step on her. One day early in January when the temperature was in the low 40s, she was flying up and down at the window while a small moth-type insect did likewise in unison with her outside the window.

Rosie spent her time at one or the other of her favorite spots at the south end of the room. That is, except when she was hunting. While Rosie looked for insects, she explored every available spot, including that portion of the sunroom which lies between the floor and the underside of the loveseat—a six-inch space more or less—and, with forward vertical movement, would float along underneath, looking for spiders.

Once, while I was feeding Rosie, she spotted a spider crawling across a large *Pachystachys* leaf and went to investigate. When the spider became aware of Rosie's presence, it scurried to the underside of the leaf and Rosie attempted to capture its silhouette. At other times, she would be drinking from the feeder that I was holding when she would stop abruptly. She would then dash across the room at a right angle and capture an insect, and immediately return to the feeder to resume taking nectar. Amazingly, she saw that bug across the room while she was feeding!

Rosie's new voracious appetite prompted me to have some extra protein for her, but for some unfortunate reason, I wasn't plagued—or blessed, as the case may be—with as many whiteflies as I've had in other years, and

Rosie would spot a dangling spider, dart over, open her beak, and devour it.

the supply in the sunroom didn't seem adequate. I'd have to bring her some from elsewhere, and the richest place for insect collecting is the basement growing area. There I was able to find some whiteflies on the undersides of the fuchsia leaves and little spiders that I carried back upstairs, dangling from their webs. Rosie, with her excellent eyesight, would immediately spot the dangling spider and dart over, open her beak, and devour it. When she ate a spider from my hand she displayed her soft, orangish gape. In an attempt to satisfy her, I would then trek back downstairs to repeat the process. It was evident that the spider supply too was being exhausted.

A local radio gardening show had a listener call in to have a small insect found near some plants and windowsills identified. The specimens collected and sent to Cornell for analysis turned out to be an unknown member of the order Diptera, which contains many small-winged fly-type insects such as fruit flies, common near rotting vegetation. My New Zealand tree fern had a number of these insects, and they were a good snack for Rosie. The little guys weren't too difficult to catch once I got the hang of it. I learned to pull my cupped hand forward and close it to catch one. I'd then carry it up to Rosie, still imprisoned in my clenched hand. When I opened my hand, the insect flew off but Rosie was incredibly fast. What took me five minutes to catch, she captured and devoured in two seconds. After two trips into the sunroom with a clenched fist, Rosie knew what I would be offering and started looking for it before it was released. On one occasion she even plucked one off my finger.

Rosie's request for insects came so frequently that I had to figure out another way to get them quicker than one or two at a time. My idea was to use a small, battery-operated hand vacuum to suck in several at once. It was wonderful: I could bring in a dozen whiteflies and several slightly larger Diptera and twist the vacuum in half, releasing the little treasures for Rosie at once. She would flit from one to another, capturing each in turn. When one landed in my hair, Rosie flew over and plucked it out with absolutely no fear. She quickly learned what the vacuum represented and would fly over to meet me any time I carried it into the room. Eventually, even the supply of Diptera was depleted. I started thinking about how I might import some insects when, around the first week in February, her appetite began to wane a bit.

On the Move—Once Rosie's desire for protein returned to its normal level, her attention turned to new spring behavior. Beginning in February, Rosie was on the move. She knew the boundaries of her room and would fly across its length at breakneck speed, do a little dip before she got to the other side, and turn around about two inches from the glass. She knew what she was doing, but because glass is an invisible barrier, she scared me when she did it. I had to do something.

Sheer curtains were the answer. Most light would be transmitted, while making her limitations more visible to Rosie. I took her in, therefore it was my responsibility to see to it that she made it through the winter unscathed. The sheers were tacked over the window frame and pulled taut. Now, if she were to inadvertently fly into the curtain, there would be some resilience there, something to bounce off. Since the south side of the room—specifically the southeast corner—was where she took off from when flying across the room, I covered the north windows and part of the east.

Since her movements seemed to parallel the time of normal migration, I had to entertain the possibility that they were significant and satisfied an instinct. The movements occurred primarily on sunny days, which may indicate that migrations occur or at least are initiated on pleasant days and not during inclement weather. Her February movements were always to the north-northeast area of the sunroom. I thought nothing of that until, after a slowdown about the second week in March, her flying shifted to the west side of the room. There are no windows on the west—only a wall—so I looked for some explanation or relevance. Perhaps the direction has something to do with the route she should have taken. By late March, the flying slowed to a trickle. Rosie's movements pretty much ended by late March, coinciding with the likely conclusion of migration.

Thinking About a Nest—Beginning much
earlier than nesting time itself, perhaps initiated by increasing day length, the gonads swell and signal the start of breeding. Since Rosie's instinctive behavior had not been altered by artificial light, she followed a natural pattern.

On its regular breeding grounds, the rufous nests farther north than any other hummingbird—from about 61° N. in Alaska and southern Yukon, south to Oregon and southwestern Montana. Nests are built on blackberry vines, on dry roots, in conifers, and in other trees and bushes. The nests are commonly built on top of old nests. Most nests are no higher than fifteen feet, with earlier nests lower to the ground. Bent reports colonies of up to twenty nests within yards of one another in second-growth vegetation.[5]

Most hummingbird nests are beautiful little structures, with mere size alone one of their most charming characteristics. The cup-shaped nest of a rufous hummingbird is less than two inches across on the outside, less than one inch on the inside, and approximately

5. Arthur Cleveland Bent, *Histories of North American Cuckoos, Goatsuckers, Hummingbirds and their Allies* (New York: Dover, 1989).

one and one-half inches high with less than one inch of interior depth. Nests are lined with soft, pale buff, cottony plant materials and moss. They are decorated on the outside with bits of bark, bud scales, moss, and lichen, and are held in place by spiders' webs. Nest construction starts in late March and April, and may take as little as one day or as much as one week to complete, if the nests of similar hummers are any indication. The white, elliptical-oval eggs, measuring approximately 13 by 8 millimeters (approximately $\frac{1}{2}$ by $\frac{1}{3}$ inch), are laid from April to July. A nesting bird usually lays two eggs, which are incubated for fifteen to seventeen days, entirely by the female.

Many of my orchids are potted in a shredded coconut-husk fiber medium and are grown in slatted cedar baskets; consequently, little strands of the fiber stick out here and there. On several occasions I noticed Rosie pulling pieces of coconut husk out of an orchid basket. She didn't do anything with them, and at first I assumed she was looking for spiders.

There are cotton sheets covering the chairs in the sunroom. They are the hospital type—more a cross between a cotton sheet and a terrycloth towel. Rosie investigated the covering and grabbed the knap in her beak and tugged on it. When she did, the covering would lift about three inches away from the chair itself. She was pulling the entire piece of material up by a thread. I wasn't sure whether she was hunting or perhaps looking for nesting material.

I began to wonder whether Rosie might be thinking about a nest. I was curious about what her reaction would be to one of a rubythroat, and was quite surprised at the result. When the nest was brought in to her, she responded differently than to any other object that I had held. I got the distinct impression she knew exactly what it was; furthermore, although definitely interested, she was quite apprehensive about it. She immediately came over to investigate and while she was checking it out, she chirped repeatedly while circling it with tail fanned and facing the nest at all times, threateningly moving from the back side of the hand that held the nest, around in a circle to the front side of my hand. I interpreted her reaction to be basically a negative one. Her posture was equivalent to a female rubythroat's threat posture, and I presume that it conveyed a similar message here. I also interpreted her loud chirp as a threatening announcement that the sunroom is her territory. And so I removed the nest.

On the last Sunday in March, when I entered the sunroom, Rosie was just leaving the southwest corner. I wondered what she might be doing, when my eyes focused on an orchid mounted on wood sparsely covered with bits of lichen. She appeared to be pecking at the lichen. Again I wondered whether Rosie was taking stock of potential nesting materials. My friend Vickie has a second home in Scottsdale. This year she brought me some pictures of two baby hummingbirds in a nest just outside one of her windows. The most unusual and surprising part was this female's choice of nesting site: an artificial outdoor sheffelera plant. If that female

Rosie gathers dryer lint for a nest.

found that site suitable, then I could see no reason why Rosie might not build hers right here in the sunroom.

I save dryer lint to offer the outdoor birds some nesting material. All-natural, undyed and unbleached cotton flannel pajamas produced the softest, purest lint I could find. I had put it aside for hummingbirds months before, but I took it out now and offered it to Rosie, placing a handful of the cottony material in between some of the lower branches on the honeysuckle plant. I couldn't help notice how warm the material became when I held it. Practically within seconds, she started gathering bits of the fluff. She flew down and, while bracing herself with her little feet, clasped a piece of the lint in her beak and yanked it away from the rest. Instead of taking off with it, she proceeded to gather more, holding on with her feet, taking additional pieces and fitting more and more in her beak

Rosie with fluff.

until the bunch of cotton was larger than her head; and
then she took off. Most of the material fell to the floor
as she flew up to a branch, and she dropped what was
left while she sat there. She visited the lint at least a
couple of times that first day. I felt sure that Rosie knew
what this plant down equivalent was for.

I didn't know whether Rosie would attempt to
complete a nest, but in case she did, I wanted to provide whatever materials she would need. Spider's web
and cobwebs are available in the sunroom, and she
could find all the moss she could possibly want on several of the mounted orchids. Although there was some
lichen here and there, my husband brought in a fallen
maple branch that was covered with soft, greenish
lichen. We placed the log in an area where Rosie could
help herself to the pieces of decoration.

On Easter Sunday, Rosie went to the fluff periodically to take a piece. Again, she didn't do anything with it, but she did do something else. Rosie had a long piece of spider's web dangling from her foot. I watched as she weaved her beak over and under the branch, back to front, as if sharpening a knife. I couldn't be sure whether she was starting a nest or just trying to remove the web. But after most of it was on the branch, she had the task of removing what remained on her foot. After a couple of fruitless attempts, she immediately went to the waterfall, chirping, fluttering, and pecking for a full two minutes. What remained of the web probably stuck to the roughish surface of the lava rock. She really kept me wondering about her nest and at that point I added some bud scales from a camellia plant to Rosie's collection of nesting material, piling them on top of the lichen-covered maple log. Each evening

Rosie weaves her beak over and under the branch when she gathers spider's web for a nest.

after returning from work I looked around to see if a nest had been started. Although I didn't find anything, Rosie did move large pieces of the lint from time to time especially late in April when finding bits of the fluff was practically an everyday occurrence.

Also, the rufous is reported to forage for midges on sandy ground early in the breeding season. On April 20, in addition to finding pieces of the fluff around, I noticed Rosie fly over to the pot of blue curls, pick up grains of sand with her beak, and literally toss them!

Spring Flowers

Rufous hummingbirds are common spring migrants in the southern California foothills and valleys, with the males preceding the females and arriving in early March just as the currants, particularly crimson-flowered currant, come into bloom. The bulk of the spring migration through central California occurs in April, where aggressive migrant rufous hummingbirds visit flowers of chuparosa, ocotillo (*Fouquieria splendens*), mints (e.g., *Stachys coccinea, Salvia spp., Satureja mimuloides*), penstemon, delphinium, tree tobacco (*Nicotiana glauca*), and other currants. Other West Coast favorites are columbine (*Aquilegia spp.*), madroña tree (*Arbutus menziesii*), paintbrushes (*Castilleja spp.*), salmonberry (*Rubus spectabilis*), and honeysuckle (*Lonicera spp.*).

I knew I couldn't duplicate all that Rosie would find in a normal spring journey northward, but I was determined to give it the best shot possible. This seemed so much more important for her spring season because she appeared to be carrying on all her normal activities.

Aquilegia formosa *is a West Coast favorite for the rufous hummingbird.*

I had wanted to offer Rosie as much as possible of what she might have encountered naturally, and a good stock of California plants proved to be the answer. Many of the California natives I had acquired for Rosie

Rosie spent much time visiting another West Coast favorite, delphinium.

during the winter came into bloom in spring. The very
beautiful romero or woolly blue curls (*Trichostema lana-
tum*), a stunning plant with fragrant foliage and deep
bluish, woolly flowers; western columbine (*Aquilegia formosa*); and the monkey flowers, *Mimulus* and *Diplacus*,
that had been so popular over the winter continued to
flower through the spring, as did the *Ribes*.

*The very
beautiful
woolly blue
curls is a
stunning plant
favored by
Rosie.*

    Ribes flowers at first glance might seem unlikely
candidates for hummingbirds because the blossoms are
so small, and one might reasonably expect a hummingbird to be most attracted to flowers similar in size to its
beak. Rosie loved all the *Ribes* species offered, returning
again and again to drink their nectar. Other flowers
you might never expect to be attractive to hummingbirds are the manzanitas (*Arctostaphylos spp.*), with an
unbelievable number of cultivars and tiny, creamy-
white, dangling, urn-shaped flowers. Rosie would cling

Rosie preferred small flowers such as the manzanitas.

Rosie and a small mint, Stachys bullata.

to the twiggy branches of this plant, at times almost upside down, to get at the nectar in the flowers, and she made numerous trips to the plant each day. One of the biggest surprises was the size of individual blos-

The small Brazilian sky flower.

One of the smallest was bumble bee plant—nothing special, just tiny.

soms most favored. She consistently preferred the smallest flowers such as the many tillandsias, *Stachys bullata*, scarlet bush (*Hamelia patens*), bumble bee plant (*Scrophularia atrata*), and Brazilian sky flower (*Duranta stenostachya*), in addition to the *Ribes* and *Arctostaphylos* already mentioned, with the single notable exception of *Passiflora,* which she loved. One of the smallest, bumble bee plant, with its one-quarter-inch green and yellowish flowers, is listed as attractive to bees. It is nothing special or outstanding as far as I can see; it was just tiny, but Rosie loved it and it brought to mind Johnsgard's comments that in Alaska, the rufous hummingbird frequently pollinates flowers more suitable for pollination by bees.

Rosie was much more attracted to Hamelia patens *than are the rubythroats*

Over the years that I've grown scarlet bush, I've noticed that although the rubythroat visits its small, tubular, orange flowers it is never with the zeal that other flowers, elicit. I've always felt that this is because of the size of each blossom, concluding that it held less nectar and must be most suitable for the smallest hum-

Mints are popular with hummingbirds and Rosie visited them frequently— here she visits Satureja mimuloides.

Salvia microphylla, *a spring mint.*

Salvia officinalis, *another spring mint.*

From time to time Rosie would make use of the dahlias.

The spring bloom of Calliandra *presents a new picture.*

mers such as the bee hummingbird (*Mellisuga helenae*) of
Cuba and the Isle of Pines. Scarlet bush is one of those
tropical plants that, like one of the California paintbrushes, hosts mites that move from flower cluster to
flower cluster and plant to plant as passengers on the

Abelia grandiflora *was a pleasant spring surprise.*

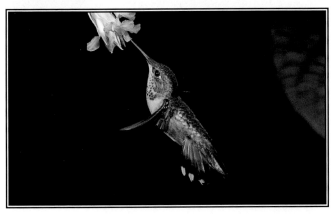

Tillandsias were her favorite.

bills of hummingbirds, even taking shelter in their nostrils. The flowers open shortly after midnight, allowing time for the mites to move in before the hummingbirds become active at dawn. Clusters of the flowers form above the leaves at the ends of the branches and are

*Rosie visits
another tillandsia.*

usually at various stages of development from buds to
mature tubes. Rosie found the single, first mature
flower on this plant within minutes of waking up, and
she wouldn't leave it alone for the rest of the day. Obviously, Rosie loved *Hamelia* flowers; again, the smallish

size of a particular flower was no deterrent.

Mints such as *Salvia*, *Stachys*, and *Satureja* are popular with hummingbirds. Rosie had flowers on *Salvia coccinea* sporadically all winter. For spring, it was joined by *S. officinalis* and *S. microphylla*. Two other spring mints, *Satureja mimuloides* and *Stachys bullata*, were in bloom and

Rosie visits Squeak's favorite, Tillandsia geminiflora.

Rosie visited them both frequently.

Squeak loved the big, bold hibiscus flowers so much he couldn't wait for them to open. Once they did open, he'd get lost in them. But Rosie acted as though they frightened her. She would approach the opened flowers to about two inches and hang there looking for a second or two, but then fly off elsewhere. I can't very well say she didn't like them; she just refused to try. Similarly, Squeak loved flowering maple (*Abu-*

tilon), but Rosie would visit it only after she had gone to everything else. But remember how Rosie showed only a passing interest in *Calliandra* during its winter bloom? The spring bloom of the *Calliandra* plants presented an entirely different picture. This time around she loved them so much that she wouldn't leave them alone, even attempting to extract nectar from the fallen flowers.

There were both disappointments and pleasant surprises in the sunroom this year. Glossy abelia (*Abelia grandiflora*), with its dainty, white, hanging bells, is a garden plant that does well under rhododendron conditions but is only marginally hardy in this area. Accordingly, abelia as a potted plant has always been wintered over in an unheated porch. This year, however, it was kept in the sunroom. The early bloom was a complete surprise and Rosie loved the blossoms visiting them frequently to drain their nectar. For quite a while, visits to abelia alternated with visits to all other flowers.

Tillandsias are interesting and attractive, make great companion plants for orchids, and are pollinated in the wild almost exclusively by hummingbirds. Of all the flowers in the sunroom, it was the tillandsias that Rosie would follow me around to get at while I was holding them. It was also the only flower she would leave the hand-held feeder for, alternating from feeder to flower, feeder to flower. Tillandsia nectar must be very special. She would find the flowers even if they were in an out-of-the-way spot.

For years I've wanted to get a photograph of one of

Each blossom of passion flower was greeted with enthusiasm.

the hummingbirds at the passion flower (*Passiflora vitifo-lia*), but could not synchronize my camera with their visits. Since it is cut back each winter, the vine, with its grapelike leaves and profuse, dramatic red blossoms, usually blooms during the summer and fall. Because of my busy schedule the past winter, I neglected to give it the usual trim and was excited to see that the plant would be in flower much earlier this year. When the first flower opened, I thought Rosie was in ecstasy, visiting that initial blossom repeatedly and chirping up a storm. *Passiflora's* only negative quality is that the flowers stay only one day, from just prior to sunrise to just after sunset. They are most beautiful as they first open and just before they close; during the bright part of the day the petals are somewhat reflexed. Nevertheless, Rosie greeted each succeeding blossom with the same enthusiasm. She would even visit passion flowers

Shrimp plant was a spring favorite.

the day after, when the buds are just about closed but there's still some nectar at the base of the petals and even in the bracts.

Rosie made her rounds among all the flowers, but when something was new, or when particular flowers first began to open, they would get special attention.

Penstemons are always popular with hummingbirds (P. spectabilis).

Once something was no longer brand-new, it became part of the route, even though fresh individual blossoms would open on the plant.

Some of the other spring flowers that Rosie enjoyed are the shrimp plant, penstemon species (*P. utahensis* being a possible favorite), columbine (*Aquilegia formosa*

Penstemon utahensis, *Rosie's favorite.*

winning hands down over the garden hybrids), and trumpet honeysuckle (*Lonicera sempervirens*). Common kalanchoe (*Kalanchoe* hybrids) was okay, but she loved trailing kalanchoe (*Kalanchoe uniflora*) and she didn't lift the blossoms as Squeak had to drain the nectar.

I was anxious to get Rosie's reaction to Mexican orchids, such as the very beautiful *Cuitlauzinia pendula*, which grows at lofty elevations of the dry oak forests of western Mexico. When the flower spike was forming, Rosie systematically removed the "nectar." When the blossoms opened, she ignored them, preferring to

Western columbine
(Aquilegia
formosa) *won
hands down . . .*

*. . . over garden
hybrids*

take the drops of nectar from behind the flowers where
they joined the spike. Spring also offered other orchids
with long flower spikes, such as *Aerides* and *Dendrobium*
and Rosie continued to find these orchid spikes to "de-
nectarize." She would hover in front of or behind them
at times, but mostly she'd hang on to something else

Trumpet honeysuckle never turned as dark indoors, but Rosie loved it anyway.

She loved trailing kalanchoe but didn't lift the blossoms to drain the nectar

Zauschneria *ordinarily blooms in late summer and early fall.*

Rosie bears down on lantana.

and stretch her neck to reach them. Typically, the orchid flowers themselves didn't appeal to Rosie.

I was able to get a few flowers on the old growth of hummingbird or California fuchsia (*Zauschneria latifolia* 'Johnstonii'), which ordinarily blooms during late sum-

Penstemon barbatus.

Rosie visits bleeding heart (note how her tail is held high).

mer and fall, and Rosie, of course, made use of them. However, she preferred western columbine to the *Zauschneria*. That really surprised me—and perhaps it is that columbine is truly a spring flower as compared to *Zauschneria*, which is noted for its importance to hum-

Rosie loved scarlet bouvardia just as much in spring as she had earlier in her stay.

mingbirds because of its late flowering; or western columbine could be a flower to which she has had more natural exposure, a "learned" flower.

Knowing which flowers to use is a learning process in hummingbirds. Young hummers try everything in the beginning; it is not something known from birth. If

Rosie was most beautiful when set against the soft lavender-blue of delphinium.

Rosie visits
Dianthus.

this is so, and columbine is a familiar flower to Rosie, it
might indicate that her first migration was correct and
that the very best thing I had done for Rosie was to buy
her familiar native plants. The fact that Squeak visited
several flowers that held no interest for Rosie might be

*What would a
garden be for a rufous
hummingbird without*
Ribes sanguineum?

because he, as an immature bird, was still learning and, therefore, willing to try more than Rosie was.

When the lantana (*L. montevidensis*) came into bloom, Rosie was in heaven—another small-flowered plant with hundreds of individual blossoms. With such a bountiful crop of flowers on one plant, I was able to observe her method of foraging. It appears that her pattern was completely indiscriminate, although she started at basically the same place on the plant regardless of where she was sitting beforehand. She would move in either a clockwise or counterclockwise, up or down, direction, not necessarily the same way twice in a row. However, she was consistent in not draining every blossom in the cluster—usually only two or three flowers per cluster were drained per visit. And when the lantana did start blooming, Rosie had a field day. As far as she was concerned, I am sure, this was what foraging was all about, flitting from lantana to fuchsia, columbine, scarlet bush, jasmine, honeysuckle, *Mimulus*, impatiens, one after another. There is no doubt that she preferred small flowers. While I can't very well say that it's conclusive about all rufous hummingbirds, it certainly was about Rosie. When given a choice between a beautiful red fuchsia with abundant flowers and the lavender lantana, she chose the tiny lantana blossoms. Her most favorite flowers of what was offered here were manzanitas, currants, and tillandsias. The only large flowers that she especially liked were passion flower, delphinium, and the beak-sized trumpet honeysuckle.

Once spring came, I went shopping at the garden center on a weekly basis. If anything was being offered for planting that I thought would be attractive, I bought it for her: delphinium, *Penstemon barbatus*, bleeding heart (*Dicentra*), as well as a new flowering quince and *Dianthus.* Flowering quince branches were also brought in from the garden. From an aesthetic point of view, Rosie looked most beautiful when set against the soft lavender-blue delphinium, probably because it brought out her rufous coloring so well. Since the ones she had in the fall weren't in flower yet, new scarlet bouvardia plants were purchased for Rosie, and she loved them every bit as much in spring as she had in the fall and early winter.

And finally, what would a garden for a rufous hummingbird be without *Ribes sanguineum?* This is the plant so timed with the return of the rufous to the West Coast. I had been unable to purchase this plant during the winter when I purchased the other *Ribes*, but found a supply for the spring and bought a four-foot pink one for Rosie. Needless to say, she wouldn't leave it alone. As with several of the other West Coast plants that were purchased, *R. sanguineum* would be planted in the garden once Rosie was released, where it would, I hoped, serve the local hummers in subsequent springs.

Odds and Ends

One of the strangest things that Rosie occasionally did was to approach a branch and while chirping incessantly, behave as though she were being stopped or held back by an invisible barrier or as if in a wind tunnel, struggling to reach the branch. After one or two seconds, she would alight in the normal manner.

A bluejay warning outside would result in an immediate halt to whatever Rosie was doing inside. She would then freeze in position with her beak held upward at an angle of approximately 45°. Occasionally I would enter her room and she'd be on a twig or on her root, frozen in place. Invariably the birds outside would be similarly frozen and patiently waiting for a hawk to leave. When she was afraid of something, such as the scraping of a snow shovel or people moving about outside, she retreated to a very low branch, six to eight inches off the floor, to hide. She seemed to be apprehensive about any overhead noise or shadows. When Rosie detected a shadow overhead, seen via the skylight, she would fly right down to about one foot above the floor, under some leaves and hide.

When she was frightened, she favored low branches and if she sensed danger, such as when the bluejays would announce the presence of a hawk, the sound of a helicopter overhead or even when my husband cleaned snow off the roof, she would cling sideways to one particular very low, but quite upright, branch. Noise must be partially to blame for her fright when a helicopter was overhead. She liked to be the loudest thing around, except for the waterfall, which she had become so accustomed to hearing that she became upset when it wasn't babbling. Although she did not like overhead sounds, rain did not produce the same reaction.

Rosie moved in and out, between and among branches and under leaves, to hide, hunt, or forage at flowers, but she never bumped into anything. She seemed to have a sense about just how much room she had and would contort her little body so she could fit into the space available.

One day Rosie was searching up and down the trunk of the sleeping hibiscus for either sap or insects. As she got near the lower portion, a dried-up leaf lying on the floor was pushed along by the breeze she had created while hovering. As she lowered herself to inspect the moving leaf, it moved some more and she followed after it. It was comical to watch Rosie follow fallen objects, such as one of her molted feathers or a fallen blossom.

A hummingbird's iris is dark brown. Their eyes are capable of both monocular and binocular vision, and

One of the few times that Rosie was willing to sit while feeding was at a tillandsia.

their eyes have two areas of sharp vision. If behavior is any indication, they appear to have excellent eyesight, not only for close focusing on flowers and insects but for distance as well, being quite capable of spotting another hummingbird, even when it is perched, at least a hundred feet away. But what's most surprising is that they may be capable of either simultaneous execution of both types of focusing or rapidly alternating between the two, as was frequently demonstrated by Rosie. While drinking from the hand-held feeder, she would spot an insect flying off to the side, and would immediately leave the feeder, capture the insect, and

Rosie would approach certain flowers and hover in front of them . . .

. . . and then would spin around and fly away without taking any nectar.

then return to the feeder. So while she was looking forward, guiding her beak in and out—binocular vision—she also appeared to be capable of focusing on what was happening to her side.

The skylight was one of Rosie's favorite places where she might sunbathe or hunt, but when the first snow fell the week before Christmas and temporarily covered the skylight, Rosie flew up there and looked at it over and over. Something was different, and she was quick to spot the change. Once some of the snow slid off the sloping skylight and Rosie was able to see new, heavy, wet snowflakes falling anew, she tried to catch them.

Rosie had many opportunities to sit while she was drinking to conserve energy, but she rarely took advantage of them. She did, however, repeatedly cling to the upright branches of *Arctostaphylos* to achieve a more advantageous position for reaching the flowers. The only other times she was willing to sit were when she was either drinking from the tillandsia or lantana flowers or taking that sweet, sticky coating from the orchid buds and spikes, at which times she'd sit on roots, plop down on stiff leaves, or hang almost upside down on wire and crane her neck to reach the desired spot.

Just as she would occasionally hover in front of a feeder as if there were an invisible barrier to stop her from approaching it completely, she would approach certain flowers and hover in front of them in a similar manner. But then she would spin around without taking any nectar and fly away. She even did this with flowers that she generally enjoyed.

Pollination of flowers that only Rosie could have had contact with is the prima facie evidence of her floral foraging. I think it's absolutely adorable when I look around at plants and find fruits forming on the currants, green berries on the *Arctostaphylos*, a large round seed on the Turk's cap, or being blinded by threads of seed falling all over me from the tillandsias.

Comparison

There are differences in all manner of natural beings except clones. Differences in individual behavior are common in the rubythroat, and one has only to watch identifiable individuals to see that certain ones are aggressive, certain ones subordinate, some more cautious, and some braver. The differences are even more noticeable among the very young.

But what makes individuals so *individual?* Squeak was such a laid-back soul, whereas Rosie was a fickle, feisty, sometimes capricious, little live wire. Squeak was the consummate creature of habit for his entire stay here. Rosie, on the other hand, was true to her habits only while they lasted. I can speculate, but I really have no idea which differences may be attributed to genera or species, which are gender-related, and which are individual behavioral characteristics. For instance, Rosie displayed much more caution. This could be a difference in species behavior, it might be sex-related, with females naturally being more cautious; or it may just be an individual trait.

I know this is Rosie's story, but I couldn't help but notice differences between her and Squeak, and would like to share some of these observations. The comparisons are neither favorable nor unfavorable. There is no *right* way to bathe, for instance, but it is interesting to see how different individuals, as well as different species, react under similar circumstances or to similar experiences and daily needs.

Rosie was a much more aggressive hunter than Squeak. Except that Squeak displayed some sexual awakening, he seemed to be relatively oblivious to nature. Rosie, on the other hand, at least gave the impression that she was very attuned to what she *should* be doing.

Whereas Squeak spent a tremendous amount of time under the fluorescents, Rosie's time there became minimal and strictly for the purposes of visiting certain flowers such as *Mimulus* or to dry off after a shower. Squeak did much more preening than Rosie, but Rosie spent infinitely more time near water, showering or in the waterfall.

Johnsgard has indicated that there's not much tail movement and, for Western species, that may well be, but Rosie displayed much more tail movement than did Squeak. Rosie's tail constantly flapped up and under her and then back and up in the air as she moved in and out at the feeder. She also held her tail higher in relation to her body than did Squeak.

As far as I'm concerned, both were little darlings.

Prospects for the Future

Quite simply, there were two alternatives with respect to Rosie's future: either she'd stay or she'd go. I wanted to know which to expect. I remembered what I had learned about Charlie and his strong territorial instincts, and speculated about what had happened with Squeak and then tried to objectively apply it to my thoughts about Rosie's future. Neither of the former birds was out of an area where he would have occurred naturally, while Rosie was totally away from her range.

Rosie appears to have followed a natural spring pattern, including movements that might have been a substitute for regular migration. But one thing Rosie didn't do for this "pseudo-migration" was gain weight. I have seen fattening rubythroats preparing for their southward migrations, and have watched fattened hummers embark on their journeys (singly and in a pair on one occasion). So if she did gain weight the amount was so negligible as to be imperceptible. By the time Rosie would be released, she might be beyond a state of migration and ready to nest. Artificial lighting didn't appear to have interfered with normal spring behavior or to have extended the short periods of diurnal activity during winter for either bird. Regardless of the lights, Rosie appeared to be totally influenced by natural solar conditions and right on schedule. Her release time would coincide with the time she should have been at her destination.

I never worried about her becoming dependent upon me. This is not a concern because of the opportunistic nature of the hummingbird, which accepts, basically, whatever comes along. Nor was I concerned about Rosie continuing her interrupted southward fall migration when she was released; that was finished business. Her options, therefore, would be either a northwest migration back to her original breeding ground or setting up a nesting territory right here in the Mid-Hudson Valley. I would have expected her to migrate back to her original nesting territory if it had been possible to release her in February, March, or even April, but her release time here might just be too late to guarantee that in May, and secretion of the hormones that initiate migration might well be over. Because of the strong homing instinct, returning to her birthplace would still seem the most natural and logical outcome, except that this is a bird that had traveled across a continent and would have to travel back at least 1,850 miles. How much time would she need?

With the first option—returning to her birthplace— the most desirable of circumstances, she might very well return here next autumn, repeating her previously successful migration. On the other hand, were she to set up a nesting territory here, I would expect her fall migration to take her, perhaps, to the Southeast, with a return trip here in spring. For Rosie's sake, the perfect resolution would be that she go back to Alaska, Canada, or wherever else her breeding territory had been and follow her genetic map. Early during her stay I had wondered if it were possible she might correct her errant way and revert to her initial route. But Calder indicates that "migration terminates with *winter site fidelity and seasonal residence*"—that winter is not one of gradual wandering but established residence. Her body had given the signal that her migration was over in September, based perhaps on the distance or duration of her journey. And odd as it may seem, her fall migration to my yard had been a successful one. Also, rufous hummingbirds recaptured close to banding locations in Georgia and Alabama in subsequent winters indicate that such is the case. Calder reports that a juvenile female rufous banded in Metairie, Louisiana, in 1988 was recaptured each winter from 1990 to 1992. He recounts similar reports for Georgia, Alabama, and Florida. In Louisiana and Alabama, wintering rufous hummingbirds were captured four to six years after banding! It is likely that these birds enjoyed a normal nesting territory. So all that would favor a return to this yard either for the winter or on her return south. I would presume that genetic information with respect to at least the maiden migration is inherited and possibly relates to a parent's successful journey. If that were so, it could mean that Rosie is the progeny of one of those birds. It might also raise the question of whether at least some related birds winter in the same locality.

As the patch on Rosie's throat would change from red to scarlet, then amber, gold, and finally greenish, as her throat changed positions in relation to my line of sight, it would remind me of another unusual summer visitor to this garden. The visit occurred in mid-July 1987, when a new male hummingbird was noticed sitting on the clothesline. His gorget was quite an unusual color, glowing from a golden orange to rosy amber, depending upon the light. At first the very different coloration was attributed to the sun, but then other things were noticed about him as well. The unusual coloration didn't stop at the gorget; his green parts were extremely dark and quite different from any of the other hummers'. And he was large, at least one-half inch larger than the others. The bird stayed with us until mid-August and then was gone as abruptly as he had come. He did not return in 1988.

I've thought about that bird many times since then, and wondered how all of that may have come about, considering the possibility of genetic misfunction. However, there's one other possibility: the bird may have been a cross between a rubythroat and a rufous. Hummingbirds have been known to hybridize and certain described species have turned out to be naturally occurring hybrids. Although the breeding range of the two do not overlap, the westernmost portions of the rubythroat's summering grounds are not that far from the easternmost portions of the rufous's. Such hybridization might account not only for the unusual gorget color but a darkened coloring overall. The larger size may well have been the result of genes or the typical result of intergeneric hybridization known as "hybrid vigor." But these are chemical and genetic questions for which I have no answers. Lynch and Ames describe two male hummingbirds found at Sacramento County, California, which later were determined to be a cross of black-chinned and Allen's hummingbirds (*Archilochus alexandri* and *Selasphorus sasin*), the same genera involved here, and cite at least ten existing hummingbird crosses as of 1970.[6] Typically, the eggs of such a mating are infertile or, if fertile, the offspring are infertile. Dr. Calder indicates that two hybrids allegedly involving the rufous cannot be accepted for sure.

It must be emphasized that hybridization between these two species is extremely unlikely. Not only is intergeneric breeding uncommon, especially among the hummingbirds inhabiting north temperate areas, it is also unlikely on the basis of geographic distribution and the fact that the rufous's habit of wandering is a postnuptial one. Although it ends quite a bit earlier, the rufous's breading season occurs concurrently with that of the rubythroat so it is possible that one of the parents of that bird may have been an off-course rufous

6. James F. Lynch and P. L. Ames, "A New Hummingbird, *Archilochus alexandri* x *Selasphorus sasin*," Condor 72:(1970)209–212.

that developed a north-south migration up and down the East Coast.

Being the eternal optimist, and in spite of all considered, I hoped that Rosie would stick around, build a nest, and produce young—and continue her relationship with me.

Release

Eventually the long winter that everyone thought (and I hoped) would never end began to melt away. As spring came and winter released its icy grip on the Northeast, I began to envision heartbreak and another bittersweet good-bye.

On April 30 I put a couple of feeders out for the rubythroats, just in case. Although the first hummer arrived May 1 in the previous year, I wasn't expecting any for at least a week, as spring this year had been an average of seven to ten days late. The weeping cherry had just begun to bloom and the apricot blossoms were still on the tree—that is, the buds that weren't frozen during the horrendous winter. I glanced over at Rosie. She was staring out the window with that "incredulous" look about her, when she would swanishly crane her neck and pull her head back as close to her tail as it will go, as though she can't believe what she is seeing. I wondered what she had seen and looked out the window myself, but I saw nothing. A short while later, a

beautiful male rubythroat appeared at one of the feeders. Could she also have seen that bird? Her behavior
after that was different. She acted agitated and "antsy"
for the rest of the day, and she became more vigorous
about nesting materials again, with a brand-new round
of gathering. She hovered under the chair and came out
with a spider's web. Then she flew over to the frayed end
of the self-tie that secures the cushion to the rattan,
grasped it, and began pulling. Next she grabbed some
more pieces of the fluff and went back to the basket to
pull out some strands of the coconut-husk fiber. When
she saw a hummingbird through the window, she would
either lower her body and extend her neck and head as if
she were going to give chase, or sail up to the window
and flutter around, vocalizing, *chip-chip-chip*. She would
then go to the different flowers in the sunroom, draining
each of its nectar. At times she would just hang in the air
with tail fanned, her version of a display. It was then that
her throat patch would become particularly brilliant.

The first hummingbird to take shelter in my sunroom, voluntarily came in for the day during Hurricane
Gloria in 1983. The door to the sunroom was deliberately left ajar. When the weather subsided, she stayed in
for a while, and each time another hummer attempted to
come in, she'd chase it and then patrol the inside of the
room, flying from window to window around all three
sides to make sure there were no other hummers there.
When she saw one, she went straight to the door, flew
out and chased the intruder, and then come back. She
knew the boundaries of the room, and Rosie did too.

On May 2, I watched as Rosie earnestly gathered even more nesting material. First she looked for spiders' webs under the chair and brought one back to a branch and began to wrap it around. Next she went under a small wooden seat and, as she approached, opened her beak to an angle of about 20° and grabbed a piece about eight inches long. But it also had some dust on it, so she brought it over to another branch and just left it dangling there. Whenever she would get a piece of web, the feathers around her head and chin would stick up and then she would stiffen and arch her body as she wrapped the web around a twig. In the beginning I had systematically removed spiders' webs whenever I found them so she wouldn't get stuck in any, but now I was sorry. Afterward she went to the cotton sheeting and began tugging at pieces of the knap again and then grabbed some additional bits of coconut-husk fiber. Something was stirring up her nesting instincts and she seemed to be shifting into a higher gear.

I thought that I had been preparing myself for the inevitable all winter, but I was wrong. While it was off in the future, it was easy to think about her departure. But now I didn't want her to leave. I was her best friend, and she didn't even know it. I thought about how she'd follow me around chirping and demanding a treat, and how we'd practically collide as she'd dart over to meet me at the feeder or the door. I smiled about all aspects of her endearing personality and lamented the fact that she had never consented to sit on my finger. I remembered how she'd have the last little nightcap while sitting on her sleeping branch. And, oh, her shower, how she loved water!

I knew I'd miss her. She had captured my heart and I was totally under her spell. Each time she'd move to the closest branch and just look at me, I could feel that little tug at my heart. It was breaking. The day of reckoning was close. She had everything here: shower on demand; the waterfall; abundant and healthy food; flowers; insects; a warm, safe, dry place to sleep; and a human who catered to her every whim. She had everything but one—her freedom. But then I thought about the nesting material. She had something to do and it was time for her to get on with her life. She was ready, but she needed her freedom. Once again I would have to be prepared, like it or not, to say good-bye forever. In spite of prior experiences, I am the eternal optimist and I approached Rosie's release accordingly.

The final consideration was what day to release her. The picture in the garden would be significantly different from what had attracted her initially. All of the flowers that beckoned her in September, the *Salvias*, *Ipomopsis*, and *Lobelia* are flowers of very late spring, summer, and fall. Now there would be less abundance. Considering the brevity of the Northeast spring and the sweeping changes that can occur during the course of one week, a few extra days would make a remarkable difference. In order to give her the best possible chance, I decided that her release would be sometime during the week beginning May 8.

Just as the first time around, it was strongly suggested that I have Rosie banded, and I thought about it
right up to the end. It was a difficult decision; there was
such a good argument in favor of banding. Here was a
bird so very far off course; information gleaned from her
travels at some time in the future could make a valuable
contribution to knowledge about the migration of the
rufous. It almost seemed the responsible thing to do.
But Rosie was an individual, a free spirit on a little
detour in life, and I had become so very fond of her that
my heart said no. Could I rely on her not being captured just because she is a banded individual? Is there
any possibility that a band would be uncomfortable or
even get caught on something? I thought about a beautiful broad-billed hummingbird that I had pho-
tographed in Arizona's Ramsey Canyon. When I had
my film developed and pictures printed, the little guy
had a band on his leg! If that went unnoticed at a distance of four or five feet, Rosie's probably would as well.

Finally, I made an eleventh-hour-decision about
banding. This could definitely benefit the entire
species. For instance, if found next or some subsequent
winter in Mexico, it would tell plenty about the bird's
ability to correct its prior mistake. It was the responsible thing to do and so I called a couple of banders. The
first man contacted in Schenectady, New York, said no,
he only bands birds captured in nets on his own prop-
erty. The second, a Sullivan County woman, could not
accommodate me because she had no small, humming-
bird-size bands. I scrapped the idea.

May 9 was a beautiful Monday morning—bright, calm, a tad cool, and relatively quiet, as are most weekdays. The forecast called for a high in the 70s and no rain. I knew it would be hard, but it had to be done. Rosie had things to do and, probably, places to go; the clock was ticking and it was time for her to leave. Ever mindful of the strong homing instinct, I had to be careful to allow sufficient time for her to complete her cycle. The rufous has a relatively brief nesting season and starts its southward fall migration earlier than other North American hummers. It was already May. Whereas every additional day she stayed improved her chances, the point would come when each additional day would be a detriment. The rest of May and all of June covers a period of sixty-three-days, nine short weeks. The nesting cycle—building through fledging—takes about six weeks and that leaves Rosie three weeks for travel. The distance from Saugerties, New York, to Cordova, Alaska, one of the farthest rufous nesting areas from here, is approximately 3,150 air miles. The closest point to Saugerties where the rufous might breed is roughly 1,850 miles. An average of those two distances— 2,500 miles—would mean that Rosie would have to travel about 119 miles per day to be on schedule. In addition, there would be several days for refueling stops. In view of the time an ordinary migration takes, it doesn't seem likely that it can be done, but late egg and departure dates can run into July and September respectively in most breeding areas.

I removed the screen from the window, set it aside, and went outside where I could coax her out if needed, as I had done with Squeak. When she saw me on the other side, she came out without any trepidation, as nonchalantly as though she had been going in and out all along. She moved to the top of the overhang and pecked a couple of times at some of last year's dried-up leaves and then flew to the chokecherry tree about twelve feet away. The loud *chip-chip-chip* as she announced her presence immediately revealed her position. The whole thing was ending before my eyes. Fresh, vivid recollections of that emotional day when I released Squeak rushed into my mind and the five years since disappeared as I relived the heartbreak as though it had happened just the day before. However, as heart-breaking and sad as it was, I must admit to not only a feeling of happiness for her but a certain heartfelt relief to see her flying free.

Rosie left the tree and flew over to the still-brown rose-of-sharon, moving from branch to branch, inspecting everything and undoubtedly enjoying her regained freedom. Then it was back to the choke-cherry. After sitting a couple of minutes more in the tree, she moved to the catalpa and inspected emerging leaves at the branch tips, moving higher and higher in the tree as she did so. "Rosie," I called, "sip, sip," the same words I used when I would offer her a treat indoors. She cocked her head and looked at me. When I repeated the string, she moved to a closer position, cocked her head, looking at me some more, as if trying to decide. Again I tried and again she moved closer. Each time I called, she got closer still, one step at a time.

After several minutes, a male rubythroat flew over to use a feeder. I turned around to look at him for a second or two, and then turned back to Rosie. She was gone and I missed her departure. My heart sunk. After that I looked and called, but I neither saw any more of Rosie nor heard her loud and distinctive *chip-chip-chip.* I knew that she had left for her nesting territory.

The feeling is hard to convey. I suppose it is best to say it was bittersweet—happy, and grateful to have spent this brief interlude together, glad that she made it, satisfied that I was able to be of help, extremely sad at the prospect of her leaving, but full of optimism about an autumnal return.

Rosie, on her last day here, sits in her tree and surveys part of her garden—perhaps imprinting for next fall.

In Retrospect

Many years ago I fantasized about a rubythroat spending a winter with me, never expecting it to become a reality. But then along came Squeak. Each time I read about an Eastern sighting of the rufous hummingbird, I wished one would pay a visit to my yard. Rosie, off course by practically the width of our continent, was my wish come true. Squeak appeared long after all the other rubythroats had migrated, right after frost claimed the flowers. Rosie appeared early but stayed. If her migration was based on the distance of her prior one, perhaps she had gone that distance. Nevertheless, and for whatever reason, Rosie did not plan to leave. I have but one little acre, more or less, in this world, and this is the second time in five years that such a visit has occurred. Who knows how many of these little birds fail to migrate or migrate to the wrong places? The numbers may be considerable.

Perhaps the most beautiful of the North American hummers, and a personal favorite, is the broad-billed hummingbird (*Cynanthus latirostris*). I read that one of these gems showed up at a feeder in North Carolina a couple of years back, and I recall thinking at the time, "I wish one would come to my yard." Well, if the past is any indication of the future, perhaps next I'll see that brilliant flash of turquoise at one of my feeders.

There were three things that Rosie loved—her flowers, her water, and her treat. I am pleased to have been able to provide her amply with what she liked best; I believe it made her stay here a positive one. At the very least, she has gotten a second chance. In his book, Dan True relates that a series of rufous hummingbirds at the San Diego Zoo all died within six months of being added to the zoo's collection, and he speculates that it is because the rufous is a "restless" bird with a need to be on the move.[7] From all outward appearances, Rosie has done exceedingly well here. If his theory is correct, then I would have to attribute Rosie's successful stay to a lack of boredom and the fact that she had been active.

7. *Hummingbirds of North America, Attracting, Feeding and Photographing*, University of New Mexico Press, 1993.

Rosie's initial visit and subsequent stay have provoked a lot of thought and I have entertained many possibilities for her future. Things may not work out as I would have it were I given the opportunity to write the script, but as long as things work out for Rosie, I'll be happy. In my heart I know there's an excellent chance she'll return in the fall, and evidence supports this feeling. But even if she doesn't, these experiences are truly what makes life rich and rewarding.